Shooting Caterpillars
in
Spain

SURVIVAL BOOKS • LONDON • ENGLAND

First published 2005

The rights of Alex Browning to be identified as the author of
this work has been asserted by her in accordance with the
Copyright, Designs and Patents Act 1988

Copyright © Alex Browning 2005
Cover illustration and cartoons © Jim Watson

Survival Books Limited
26 York Street, London W1U 6PZ, United Kingdom
(☎ +44 (0)20-7788 7644,🖺 +44 (0)870-762 3212
✉ info@survivalbooks.net
💻 www.survivalbooks.net
To order books, please refer to page 266

British Library Cataloguing in Publication Data.
A CIP record for this book is available
from the British Library.
ISBN 1 901130 49 5

Printed and bound in Finland by WS Bookwell Ltd.

ACKNOWLEDGEMENTS

My sincere thanks to Joe and Kerry Laredo and Graeme and Louise Chesters who planted an idea, and especially to Graeme who pruned it, Jim Watson who brought all his skills to bear on the cover and illustrations, and Di Tolland for her enthusiasm and hard work.

My special thanks go to Peter Read who has been a rock throughout, and without whom the idea could never have become reality.

Alex Browning

THE AUTHOR

As a child Alex Browning was dragged around from pillar to post by her gypsy parents, who sailed round the world for their honeymoon and never quite got the hang of farming on dry land. She went to a Catholic boarding school in Wales and spent many years arguing with the headmistress about her lack of faith and homework. She was expelled, several times, usually for smoking – but on one occasion for bringing her pregnant horse to school and cutting lessons to attend the birth.

She has the attention span of a fruit fly and consequently had many jobs, which have included nightclub hostess, interior decorator, working on a provincial newspaper, furniture factory machine-minder, auxiliary nurse and reader for a publisher.

In her turn she dragged her long-suffering husband around Somerset restoring properties, before hauling him (and their two cats) off to Spain. They had little money and very fuzzy ideas on how to make a living: *Shooting Caterpillars in Spain* is the warts-and-all account of their life in Spain.

> **Pet lovers can rest assured that the author doesn't condone the massacre of Spain's wildlife – the caterpillars in question transmit a poison that can prove fatal to cats and dogs.**

CONTENTS

1. Throwing Your Heart Over   11

2. The Goat Wife   23

3. Napoleon Lives!   39

4. The Water Fairy   53

5. Caterpillar Wars   69

6. Friends & Neighbours   85

7. Cosmic, Man!   97

8. Mountain Krauts   111

9. A Death, and a Life   123

10. Recovery   135

11. The Snail Men   149

12. El Gato Macho   163

13. Goodbye to the Captain 177

14. The Last White Queen of Sarawak 181

15. Up, Up and Away 195

16. Parrot Pie 207

17. A Literary Soiree 223

18. The Pink Palace of Jaipur 233

19. The Augean Stables 245

20. The End of the Beginning 257

With fondest love and heartfelt thanks to

Chris, Hope and Peter.

Without you this story could not have been told.

INTRODUCTION

Alex Browning and her husband James were becoming bored with their comfortable but staid life in Somerset and needed a new challenge. Buying a Volvo was proof that terminal middle-age wasn't far away, so in a moment of temporary insanity they (and their cats) chucked it all in for a new life in a leaky, snake-infested farmhouse in southern Spain.

Alex and James are practical people who can turn their hands to (almost) anything, but their new life turned out to be a constant, almost vertical, learning experience. With virtually no spare funds, the enormity of what they had taken on was daunting, and almost every tentative step forward was followed by two steps backwards. However, with the help of friendly but eccentric neighbours and expat friends, who ranged from the odd to the disturbed and downright criminal, they somehow managed to stay afloat.

Their attempts to start a farmhouse holiday business – a world away from the beaches, burger bars, discos and souvenir shops that many holidaymakers yearn for – weren't helped by having no telephone, weather which ranged from ferociously hot to terrifyingly stormy, Kafkaesque bureaucracy, pernicious lawyers, a house full of mentally unstable cats and alarming wildlife, constantly expiring cars, medical emergencies and personal tragedies, not to mention a looming recession that would have serious repercussions for Spain's tourist industry.

How Alex and James survived is a heart-warming tale of triumph and disaster that will keep you engrossed, and their amusing (and occasionally heart-rending) experiences – and the escapades of their pets – will have in tears of laughter.

1.
Throwing Your Heart Over

It all started the day Pogo stole the little girl's cake. That was the day the rot set in, the canker of dissatisfaction that can spoil your life, or lead to a very different life that stretches your mental and physical sinews; a life that brings you close to the edge of hunger and danger, a life that gives you that 'Wow, Life is Wonderful!' feeling.

Pogo, the trigger to all this existential navel gazing, was a large, greedy bay horse who played an important part in our lives, as my husband James and I both enjoyed riding and competing in horse trials. This particular morning, when Pogo became a perpetrator and I saw the light, started normally enough as we clattered out of the stable yard into the main street of Bower Hinton, a Somerset village that had been pleasantly sleepy and rural for the previous thousand years or so. Geese foraged on the green in front of Mouse Cottage, our lovingly restored hamstone house, and the horses grazed in a rented cider apple orchard beside the house.

'Morning Phil – your damn geese chased me down the garden again and I had to hide behind Pogo,' I called out to our neighbour, who laughed unfeelingly.

'Ay, thiccy birds can be a bit fierce, especially that ol' gander, gotta keep a broom handy for 'ee... you be wanting some duck eggs today my lover?'

Phil and his wife were good neighbours: typical Somerset farmers, they were a generous, good-natured family always ready with a joke or advice.

The sun was hot on my back as I pulled Pogo up at the red traffic light in the narrow village high street and my attention wandered to the perfectly tended gardens and hanging baskets of a village engaged in the 'Somerset in Bloom' competition. Sensing the slack hand on the reins, Pogo struck without warning, thrusting his snout through the open window of the car alongside, snatching a cream and jam doughnut from the hand of the little girl sitting in the back seat. The child howled with terror as Pogo munched her cake, his head bobbing up and down with relish. Suddenly he sneezed, spattering the car with gobs of cream, jam and green phlegm. Unfortunately, the passenger window was also open this hot morning, and the girl's mother caught most of it across her carefully made-up face and immaculate white blouse.

This was too much and father leaped out of the car shouting and waving his fist at Pogo who, being a nervous horse despite his large size, recoiled and defecated copiously.

Mother also got out of the car to give me a piece of her mind, stepping straight into the steaming pile of horse poo in her strappy high heels.

'F****** horses,' she screeched, 'shouldn't be allowed in the f****** countryside, doing their f****** turds in public, it's f****** disgusting, something should be f****** done about it.' She paused to catch her breath and shake some poo off her foot.

'Look, I'm really sorry,' I said, 'he doesn't usually do this sort of thing, let me get your daughter another cake. Here, maybe a tissue will help...'

'As for you, you snooty f****** bitch,' she snarled, 'sitting up there like the f****** queen on that bloody horse...'

The lights had turned to green for the second time and drivers further back in the queue who couldn't see what was going on were now hooting. Father, who looked like he might have hypertension, waved his fist at them as well as Pogo, who was backing away from his tormentors.

A gentleman in a pork-pie hat pushing his wheelchair-bound wife on the pavement was now threatened by the huge incontinent bottom. Being true country people they weren't nervous of the horse, but didn't care for bad language.

'Oooh, it's a real shame how some people carry on over nothing and such language in front of the kiddy!' remarked the wheelchair lady with pursed lips.

'Right, love, frightening t'orse like that.' Pork-pie laid the callused calming hand of a man well used to horses on Pogo's sweaty neck. 'Should know better.'

'Don't you criticise my wife, you old fart!' howled father, turning on pork-pie.

This, I realised, was how wars started. It was quite easy to see how a small incident like a stolen cake could have terrible consequences. In the interests of civic calm, I dismounted and tied Pogo to the railings, before grovelling all round and giving the family, whose day I had apparently ruined, five pounds to buy another cake.

By the time I got back to Pogo he had alleviated *his* emotional distress by leaning over the railings and eating most of Mr Trecockle's prize blooms. I looked in horror at the couple of marguerites still revolving in his sugar and jam frosted lips, but worse was to come as dear old Mrs Trecockle limped out and looked at the carnage.

'Don't yew worry, my dear,' she piped, her liver-spotted lips trembling. 'Accidents will happen. Fred 'as got some more flowers out back in case o'summat ruinin 'is display – powerful keen 'e is on t' 'Somerset in Bloom' contest.'

I trotted home in a subdued mood. The country didn't feel like the country any more with the influx of grockles (Somerset slang for tourists or strangers) to our little village. What had once been cow-parsley and cowpat-splattered country lanes with the occasional unhurried car, or a farmer herding cows on a bicycle, had become racetracks for frenzied Londoners in Chelsea tractors searching for twee weekend cottages. These busy people didn't like to be kept waiting, so riding, bicycling or walking the dog were fast becoming extreme sports for us slow-moving peasants.

Most city-dwellers, and especially Londoners, seemed to think that living in a rose-smothered country cottage would transform their lives; that all the wrinkles would be smoothed out once they were on the rural Highway to Happiness. Our personal highway to happiness had petered out, both literally and figuratively, on a roundabout in a new housing estate.

Developers had bought our rented apple orchard and were planning a further estate of executive homes to match the one along the lane. All over Somerset the rows of gnarled cider-apple trees were being felled to make way for rows of identical jerry-built boxes, and our way of life was disappearing as fast as the apple blossom.

Mouse Cottage was nearly completed after three years of backbreaking work and it felt like time for a new challenge. James and I started playing the 'what if' game. What if we could sell the cottage for a good profit and start our own business? What if we moved abroad? It was an exciting scenario, only spoilt by one hard fact; we had little capital between us and no prospects of getting any more except by hard work. On the plus side, James was a highly skilled engineer and had hands-on building experience, while I could also hold up my end of an RSJ, decorate, cook and garden.

It's impossible to say how we make decisions, on what hidden level the dialogue takes place, but we all know when a decision has been made. Reason doesn't necessarily have much to do with it, nor does the opinion of one's elders, betters or family. Suddenly you reach a crossroads where you have to make a momentous decision; it can be scary; it probably *should* be scary. With hindsight you can see those nodes and wonder what would have been the outcome if you had taken a totally different course of action, but of course you can never go back. Once past the 'shall we, shan't we' point you must have courage and pursue your dream.

Horse riders coming up to a big and frightening fence have a choice: stop and turn away or go for it. If you go for it with conviction, if you 'throw your heart over' as the Irish say, your body and horse will follow (not necessarily in the correct order of course).

On these shaky grounds we decided to throw our hearts over the fence. It was time for a new road in some warm, convivial European country. We left our jobs, threw a monumental going-away party, sold all the junk with a garage sale and set out for Spain in a Tonka truck (a tiny Toyota Hi-Ace) with just the bare necessities of life and two seriously unhappy cats wailing for their Mouse Cottage. We felt like wailing with them as we drove through the drizzle to the ferry. Already I missed my lovely, brave horse who'd fought his way back from a crippling back problem to give us endless fun in competition and endurance rides. I'd taught James to ride on him and seen him go from total novice to intermediate trials rider in less than two years, despite some crashing falls. The only consolation was the old horse had gone back to his previous owners in Rutland who were prepared to give him a luxurious retirement home.

As I had friends in southern Spain and had spent many happy holidays there, the Costa del Sol was the obvious choice. A house-hunting visit before totally burning our boats narrowed the area down to Alhaurin el Grande (Alhaurin means 'The Garden of Allah' in Arabic), a small town in the hills west of Malaga. Property here was cheaper than on the coast, it was an attractively verdant area, as the Moors had discovered, and it seemed ideal for the business we were planning: farmhouse holidays for those who preferred the quieter pace of life with opportunities for bird-watching, painting, riding, walking, or simply lying inert beside a pool.

For the exploratory visit to Alhaurin el Grande, I had asked my Spanish-speaking friend Paddy to come with me for moral support and as translator when my Beginner's Class Spanish failed me. The narrow potholed road from Mijas, with its total lack of guard-rails on switchback curves and free-fall drops, made Paddy extremely nervous. At first this made me laugh, but I wasn't laughing so much after glimpsing the third or fourth wrecked car several hundred feet below.

Feeling better after a jolt of coffee and a pacharan, we went to meet Diego, an estate agent I'd contacted from England. He'd advertised that he spoke English, but half an hour later I wasn't so sure. He spoke machine-gun fast and loud, with more hand-ballet than a Thai dancer, but few of his sentences made any sense. However, Paddy assured me his Spanish asides were intelligible and he was certain he could find a suitable property for us.

The rest of the day was an eye-opening, butt-clenching tour of hopeless properties. Some had fantastic views, perched on mountainsides that would make a goat nervous, while others were one-bedroom, concrete shackettes built for weekending Malagueños to tend their citrus trees, which had views of – well – citrus trees. Suitable villas with a pool and four to six bedrooms were far too expensive, totally out of our reach. The available *fincas* (farm or smallholding, typically under ten hectares) on Diego's books, although they had land – in some cases whole mountainsides – tended also to have rising damp, falling damp and the sort of plumbing that would have been familiar to our great-grandparents.

It puzzled me why there was usually a rampart of prickly-pear cactus surrounding farmhouses, until Diego explained the finer botanical points of *opuntia*: not only does the plant act as an impenetrable fence against animals and unwelcome visitors, it also rapidly processes and deodorises bodily waste, and you can also eat the fruits of your labour, so to speak. The only downside to this biological miracle is the fine irritant hairs covering the fruit – should you inadvertently impale yourself, you will spend many hours of embarrassment and agony having the near invisible spines removed.

Diego drove with great verve and machismo, giving us a running commentary as he slewed around bends over sheer drops, bumped over boulders in dry riverbeds and hurtled down mule tracks. This was bad enough, but he liked to make his conversational points with eye contact, especially with Paddy, who was huddled in the back wearing impenetrable black shades and making little whimpering noises.

The first day we didn't see anything even remotely suitable, which made us feel even more stressed. One 'delightful rustic property' was an ex-chicken farm on a featureless plain, dotted with dead and dying fruit trees. The house was so full of rubbish we had to sidle through the rooms sideways, while trying to keep our hands and clothes away from the dusty grease that coated every surface. It seemed the source was the kitchen, a stygian cave where the walls, ceiling, floor and cabinets had a strange texture, almost rubbery, with a stove that looked more like a gigantic melting black candle than an appliance. A sweetish-burnt smell, like an essence of bird fried in rancid oil, still lingered on the stuffy air. The poor chickens had obviously all ended their miserable lives being sacrificed on this altar to the fry-up before the owners had retreated back to England penniless. Even Diego's enthusiasm was slightly muted as he assured us that the house was being sold fully furnished, 'as you seed it'.

I found out later about the dead trees, as did the many foreigners who bought cheap properties in the area around Cartama, only to discover that the water supply was not only unreliable, but also saline. There had been so much abstraction from the aquifers that salt water from the sea several miles away had seeped into the water supplies, corroding pipes, killing plants and making your cuppa taste vile.

Before seeing the next property, we stopped to have lunch at a bar in Torre Alqueria. Diego ordered a selection of *tapas* and a jug of *sangria* to keep us going, which was most welcome. He asked if there was anything I didn't like. This was quite easy really as I like everything, bar tripe and strong salami-type sausages. Paddy wolfed down a little dish of a brown stew called *callos*, smacking her lips enthusiastically. When I asked what it was, she winked at Diego before telling me it was just a stew made with chickpeas in a savoury gravy; it sounded good, so they ordered another dish which I tried – it was delicious and soon disappeared. They looked at each other and tittered.

'What's so funny?' I asked suspiciously.

She giggled. 'That stew, the *callos*, is tripe.'

I wondered whether to feel queasy, but it seemed easier just to accept that I actually liked tripe Spanish-style, and the *sangria* helped. Refortified, we got into Diego's car and headed out of the village, which was comparatively new and laid out on a grid system, with groups of houses facing onto a shared gated courtyard. It felt more Moroccan than Spanish, with the windowless backs of the houses turning blank walls to the street. It had a strangely secretive sullen atmosphere, which made Paddy and I a bit uncomfortable, but Diego dismissed our twittering and told us it was one of 'Franco's villages', built on the dictator's orders as social housing during the '50s. Soon we had left the houses and were weaving across a grid of pockmarked roads, with the remains of lamp-posts, wrecked electricity boxes, gaping manholes, and goats and dogs nibbling lethargically at heaps of rubbish – it looked more like a war zone than a village.

After a few minutes drive, the houses vanished and we were on a winding grass track which segued into a dry riverbed, shouldered with rock formations. Sometimes the track was beside the river, sometimes it wandered into the river and out the other side, but always it angled upwards. And upwards. Now there were quite respectable mountains on either side and Paddy was having a *crise de nervios* each time we slid sickeningly across the track after hitting a rut or large stone. There were several old farmhouses spilling down the slopes, each with a large beehive-topped wellhead and boundaries snaking across ravines and up nearly vertical scree, delineated by whitewashed boulders and the odd tree. Although they obviously had water, they didn't appear to have anything else: there were no fields, no crops, no visible animals.

Diego told us that water, strangely enough, wasn't a problem in the bone-dry mountains: you just employed a water-diviner to find a spring, the *pozo* man came with his drilling equipment and shortly you would have a stream of cool, crystal-clear water. He couldn't, however, tell us how they built the wells before modern drill rigs were used, or indeed what the farmers produced in this barren land.

'Chickens, goats, ribbits might be?' He shrugged. It was all a bit academic, as most of the farms seemed to be deserted. We bumped and slewed around a final corner and were almost at the top of the mountain before Diego stopped before a fancy wrought-iron gate leading to a grass-carpeted gravel drive and a neat two-bedroom villa. Looking back down the mountain, there was an eagle's eye view of Malaga and the coast, and we gawped at the million-dollar view, breathing air so pure and knife-keen one could feel the breath sliding in and out of lungs and sinuses.

The house was a disappointment: not only was it tiny, it was so low-ceilinged James would have to shuffle around with his knees bent, and there wasn't enough room to extend. There were 182 steps leading down to the well, so deep a dropped stone returned only the faintest of plops, long after one had given up listening. Some vines were grimly hanging on to a non-productive life and the pigsties gave the clue to what else the previous owners had done for a living. It was a lovely little doll's house on the roof of the world and I would have liked to buy it as a retreat, a place to write, paint and think. But to judge by Paddy's reaction, it might not get the thumbs-up from our putative paying guests, to say nothing of their car hire companies – if, after heavy rain they had to breast a raging torrent booby-trapped with sump-breaking boulders. Come to that, I wasn't sure I wanted to yomp the groceries up 1,000 vertical feet if the car broke down, so we crossed it off the list.

'I heave tree houses for youse today.' Diego said as he greeted us enthusiastically with a volley of kisses when he collected us from the hotel the next day. He set off towards Coín at the usual whirlwind pace, turning so suddenly off the road onto what looked like a goat path that for a moment we were airborne, to a chorus of surprised screams from Paddy and I.

'Yew boats shouldn't be frotted,' Diego remarked. 'This track's a beech, but yew boats okay wid me.'

The sylvan leitmotif to Diego's speech was beginning to get me down, as was his driving and the two dreary shacks we had seen that morning, both with scrawny half-starved dogs tethered outside as a cheap form of security; most Spaniards are terrified of dogs. Apparently, it was normal to leave the dogs chained up all week, with maybe a couple of visits to feed them chicken carcasses. But it was difficult to see the point, because, with the dog securely chained at the front of the house, a quadriplegic on Mogadon could have broken in at the back.

We now had only one more property to see.

'Thees is a wonnerful house I show, yew wood love it at once for the *vista*, but vary expensive from theese Danish, how yew say, les bion lady,' Diego remarked.

For once, he was right. Finca Tara was perched on the edge of a bluff overlooking a spectacularly beautiful green valley with a backdrop of mountains. The only signs of habitation were a couple of tiny whitewashed shacks half hidden by trees on the slopes opposite. Below us hoopoes *popopo*'ed as they looped in their curious catenary flight into the eucalyptus trees. We examined the house: it was too small and had no pool, telephone or garden. The wiring was pathetic, as was the plumbing. Walking through the front door, the first sight that greeted you was of a yucky brown, none-too-clean lavatory, followed by an abominable kitchen with '60s pseudo-wood formica cabinets, set off to perfection by virulent orange tiles. The water came from a rat-infested well in the three-acre olive grove 200 feet below, and we couldn't afford it anyway – in short, it was perfect.

2.
The Goat Wife

It was Christmas Eve, and we were sitting on the terrace of *our finca*. Well, technically it was still Ulla's *finca* as she had given us a 'mortgage' as part of the deal, but we had made the emotional and financial commitment. With glasses of *cava* in hand, we pondered the huge step we'd taken. On the face of it, there was no contest: at 5pm on Christmas Eve in England it would be dark, cold and probably raining on the scurrying crowds of frenzied last-minute shoppers. While they were being tempted by festive bumper packs of toilet rolls decorated with holly leaves, we were sitting admiring the mauve and dove greys of the Serranía de Ronda mountain range in the far distance. Closer to hand the soft tones strengthened into the rich winter palette of green and gold spiked with citrus orange that swept down from the foothills and into our valley.

The valley, although cultivated, was otherwise unmarked by civilisation. There were no power pylons or telegraph poles, no metalled roads or street lights, just a couple of whitewashed *casitas* used by families who lived in the town, but liked to nourish their peasant roots by working the land at weekends.

From our perch on the edge of the bluff the land fell away steeply to the deep, narrow *río* (more of a stream) that marked our southern boundary, with the little tiled well house on the bank almost hidden by eucalyptus and poplars. Native Americans call the poplar 'the noisy tree' because it shivers and rustles its silvered leaves in the slightest breeze, but they were silent now in their winter nakedness.

On the other side of the *río,* our neighbour Antonio's *huerta* was a model of neatly pruned fruit trees stockinged with whitewash, and rows of ordered vegetables grown both to feed his family in Malaga and to produce income. Every week he loaded his van and took produce to the village shop in La Cabra and to the market in Alhaurin el Grande, earning barely enough to provide the necessities of life for himself and his aged father.

The hillside facing us was mostly dotted with gnarled and heavily-productive olive trees, the soil around them harrowed into swirls as intricate as the raked gravel of a Japanese Zen garden. Dotted here and there were glossy-leaved citrus orchards and tiny vineyards, just large enough to provide for family and friends, and the odd stranger within the gates.

Salvador's land, which was just within sight, looked different: perhaps because he was younger than Antonio and had more enlightened ideas. His patch featured artichokes and asparagus, apricots and kakis. Salvador had paid us a visit within hours of our arrival, bringing a present of leeks fresh from the earth.

'*Bienvenido*, why are you here, are you rich?' he enthusiastically shook hands, leaving muddy smears on our comparatively clean fingers. It was our first experience of the disconcerting Spanish directness; if they wanted to know something, they asked.

'No, Salvador – we aren't rich, we're here to work.' We did our best to explain what we hoped to do, but Salvador looked increasingly baffled.

Finally he grinned and shook his head. 'Nobody would want to come here for a holiday; they only want the sea and sand down on the coast! But if you need anything, I'm across the valley.' He pointed at some terracing. 'The house is behind those trees, but mind the dog, he is *muy feo.*' Salvador bounded down the slope and jumped the stream, turning for a last wave.

Although the *finca* was only a mile from the village of La Cabra, four miles from Alhaurin el Grande and 12 miles from Malaga, this was Andalucia at its most rural. Our little valley was a microscopic wrinkle in a much larger altiplano, the fertile bed of a monstrous Cretaceous estuary bracketed between two mountain spines, the peaks of long-extinct volcanoes a reminder that this was seismically-active territory, with fault lines running from Antequera to Granada and out into Malaga Bay. The last big earthquake – which killed or injured over 2,000 people in the Malaga region – was a mere 100 years ago, geologically less than the blink of a Tyrannosaur's eye.

But back to Christmas Eve. We'd had enough bubbly to find everything cosmic: the crystal clear air, the saturated colours of the countryside, and the alien smells and sounds. The addition of a flaring sunset of carmine, saffron, regal purple and apple green simply added icing to the wow factor.

We were brought back to earth with a bump by the sound of a cat being copiously sick. Smoo, the Imperial Rabbit, had chosen our bed to regurgitate assorted lizard body parts and his supper. He was a very British sort of cat; a large stocky tabby with spectacular markings on model-glossy fur. Reserved, cautious and, in general, picky about his food, he didn't cause much trouble – except when he had to go to the vet. Keeping him in a cat carrier was like trying to keep mercury in a string bag. He didn't like being petted, but decided for himself when an emotional one-on-one was called for, and his victim had to submit to a hot'n'heavy needle-clawed lap squat as he lay rigid and awkward as an encyclopaedia on one's punctured knees.

I didn't scold him about the lizard as the sea voyage and journey through Spain from Santander had been as hard on him as on us. This was his way of saying he was upset in the full sense of the word, whereas young Luigi, a small black cat with a waiter's immaculate white shirtfront and white socks, was much more upbeat. He'd been luxuriating in the sun all day and exploring his new territory. Hardly more than a kitten, he had no preconceived notions about *his* world.

On Christmas Day we were awakened by hot sunshine spearing through the curtains and took our breakfast on the terrace. The contrast between the England we had just left and this warmth and light filled us with enthusiasm and energy, and we were going to need all of it to get Finca Tara open by April as the farmhouse holiday business we had planned. Ulla, the Danish lady from whom we'd bought the *finca* was a delightful person, but even she would have admitted that it was in a hell of a state.

James spent Christmas morning unblocking the only toilet,

while I scrubbed the unappetising kitchen. Our furniture wouldn't arrive from England until later in the month, but Ulla had sold us the house part-furnished, so we didn't have to worry about the necessities.

I found a box of Christmas decorations in a cupboard, cut a big olive branch and stuck it in a bucket as a Christmas tree, covered with pretty, unfamiliar Scandinavian baubles and dollies that looked freshly festive. We had plenty of seasoned olive wood so a sumptuous fire was laid in the beehive fireplace in the corner of the sitting room – the house felt like a refrigerator as soon as the sun dropped below the horizon.

It was time to go up to La Cabra and phone parents and friends in England. The only public phone for miles around was cunningly situated in Juan's Bar, which was a corrugated-iron roofed shack tacked on to his house. Juan was the local entrepreneur and also the Gaz depot, and domestic life revolved around the *bombona* (gas bottle), the heavy, awkward, rapidly emptying bane of life that provided hot water and cooking for most people, even in towns.

Juan's *übershed* was packed as tight as a barrel of salted cod, and the uproar fell to a whisper as the word went around that the new *guiris* (foreigners) were present. James and I longed for the ground to open up as we stumbled through a greeting and request for coffee and the use of the telephone under the unabashed and inquisitive stares of everyone present. Juan replied with a torrent of words in an accent so brutally thick that we understood *nada*. It bore no resemblance whatsoever to the careful Castilian Spanish we had been trying to learn in evening class: for all practical purposes he might as well have been speaking Swahili. It was so hopeless I just switched off – when miraculously what he was saying began to make sense. This intuitive listening proved to be the key; don't listen to the words, just let the meaning filter into a blank mind. This technique certainly helped understand what was being said *to* us, but unfortunately it didn't help in the slightest when it came to

27

making ourselves understood in Spanish.

A magnificently upholstered lady in a reindeer-and-Santa patterned woolly was chattering in Spanish on the phone. Finishing her call, she introduced herself as Janet. She and her husband Don had been living in La Cabra for over ten years and knew all there was to know about the place, even how to use the phone for overseas calls.

'Good luck, it can be difficult making an overseas call this time of year,' Janet warned sympathetically. 'Telefonica only has a limited number of international lines, and remember, you must keep talking to yourself or whistling while you wait for the connection; if there's silence on the line for more than 15 seconds it will automatically cut off – must go, we'll see you around, byee.'

The phone had been thoughtfully sited between two beeping, clanging fruit machines and the TV at full blast, and Juan's patrons had gone back to simultaneous shouting, which is the Andaluz form of polite conversation. The revellers greeted newly arrived friends and neighbours with welcomes that would have been excessive between close relatives parted under duress for many years. Added to which, the tin roof of the bar magnified the sound making your eardrums bounce, so when we finally did make a connection the conversation mostly consisted of 'Sorry, say again?' and 'Whaaaat?'

The news from my mother was distressing: her little whippet, Kipper, had died on the day we left England. I could imagine how she felt this Christmas morning and left the bar in tears, feeling miserable and guilty that I couldn't be there with her.

Without Kipper we might not even have become a couple: she broke the ice for James the first time I took him home to meet my parents. I'd been nervous about this meeting on several counts, as my father was a notoriously peppery ex-cavalry man, and my mother could be unpredictable after a drink or two, especially when it came to my boyfriends. James was not only quite a lot younger than me, he was also penniless, divorced and had two daughters.

Having greeted James, my father handed him a sherry and started interrogating him about his prospects, much to our joint embarrassment as he didn't have any; besides, our relationship hadn't reached the commitment stage and he certainly wasn't about to ask papa for my hand in marriage.

During this excruciating examination Kipper had been snuffling around on her knees, her long snout beneath a bookcase. With a squeal and a scuffle a large rat broke cover and made for the door, and being a sporty little whippet she made a grab for it. Unfortunately the rat grabbed back, fastening it's fangs into her lip, and all hell broke loose as the animals fought tooth and nail, both screaming like banshees.

My father gave a great roar: pulling his cavalry sabre off the wall, he danced around the combatants waving the sword in whistling arcs as he tried to stick the rat, with mother cursing him like a navvy as she dodged in and out, trying to save her ornaments from being swept off the mantelpiece and her dog from a spectacular Japanese-style beheading. Thankfully, Kipper got a grip and killed the rat before my papa trashed the drawing room, and we had another drink and relaxed, the inquisition forgotten. James looked completely stunned and I hardly dared tell him that both the interrogation and the sabre waving would qualify as routine behaviour in my family.

The rats, which came from the barn next door, were also par for the course, and on one occasion when my mother pulled open the plate warming drawer under the stove, her dinner guests were bemused when an entire rat family leaped out and scuttled off through the cat flap.

Still thinking about our loved ones in England, we walked back to Finca Tara and let the cats out. Luigi wandered off into the garden in his usual inquisitive way, while Smoo settled down on the terrace for a wash and brush-up, back leg cocked in the air. The evening birdsong was abruptly halted by a piteous scream from behind the garden wall and Smoo leapt up and hurdled the five-foot wall like a tabby Exocet. There followed another dreadful wail in a rather lower register and a lot of scuffling. Looking over the wall I saw Luigi nursing a badly bitten paw and Smoo, with blazing eyes and a great chunk of fur in his mouth, seeing off a large ginger tom with a bare bottom. The ground was covered in enough ginger fur to stuff a pillow and I hoped the tom had learnt his lesson. It was surprising that Smoo had gone to Luigi's defence, as they didn't get on that well, but he seemed on better terms with the younger cat after this incident. The ginger bully sloped off over the track to our neighbour Antonio's house, where he lay low to plan his next assault.

We had met Antonio briefly when Ulla introduced us to our neighbours on the *acequia* (large-scale irrigation system of water channels in multiple ownership) road. He had seemed welcoming enough and waved whenever we passed him as he worked on his vegetables or moved his goats, always accompanied by his friendly little dog Pito, which looked like a long-tailed corgi. On fine mornings we glimpsed Antonio's elderly father sitting outside the front door for his airing. I was expecting to see a Señora Antonio and, sure enough, one morning there was a woman with long wavy brownish-grey hair leaning over the top of the stable door that faced our garden-to-be. I waved and called out *'Buenos días, Señora,'* and was surprised when she didn't respond. Maybe she's a bit deaf, I thought, or doesn't see too well.

The next morning she was there again and this time I went overboard waving and yodelling *'Buenos días'* – but still she ignored my friendly overtures. I didn't know whether to be hurt or annoyed. Maybe she just disliked foreigners, but it seemed strange when Antonio was so friendly.

At coffee time James came in from pruning the trees down on the land and I mentioned my social failure to him. 'I can't understand it,' I moaned. 'Mrs Antonio won't even give me the time of day. Do you think she doesn't like foreigners or something?'

'Mrs Antonio? Are you sure that's Mrs Antonio? Where did you see her?'

'The last two mornings she's been leaning over the stable door at the back of the house. I waved and said hello but she just ignored me!'

James looked at me blankly for a moment and then guffawed until tears came into his perfect 20/20 blue eyes. He's a man who doesn't guffaw, or even laugh aloud often, so I sat there puzzled, beginning to get annoyed.

'Go and put your glasses on,' he finally spluttered, 'and have another look at your Mrs Antonio, you goose.'

I put on my spectacles, which I normally don't wear from a mixture of vanity and inability to find them, and went out into the garden. Suddenly all was embarrassingly crystal clear: the fuzzy figure was in fact a monstrous billy-goat standing with its front hooves hooked over the stable door, lush falls of brown and caramel hair framing inscrutable amber eyes, as he gazed with rapt attention at his new neighbours.

I never did get to the bottom of why Antonio was unmarried, as single men of marriageable age don't last long in Spanish society, where the extended family takes pride in ensuring that the next generation is wedded and bedded. (Although for some reason the Spanish birth rate has fallen to such an extent that it's now among the lowest in the world.) His family came from Malaga in a fleet of vans most Sundays to eat the produce of the *finca* and socialise, and the chattering and shrieks of laughter went on for most of the day.

When a family van reached the end of its life, instead of scrapping it or ripping off the plates and abandoning it at a beauty spot like any normal Spaniard, Antonio pensioned them off like old carthorses and lined them up nose to tail in the entrance to his *finca*. No doubt he enjoyed stroking his old favourites, like the ca.1945 Seat panel van apparently made from flattened dustbins. They made a nice screen to shield him from prying eyes, but unfortunately they were the first thing we saw when we came out of our front door. I planned to make an orchard and garden in the quarter acre of flat ground that lay between the house and Antonio's *finca*, with tall trees as a boundary to block off the worst of the van graveyard. Sadly it would take at least three or four years before the trees were tall enough to make any appreciable difference, but we had to start somewhere.

The entrance to Finca Tara also needed some work: Ulla had erected a steel water-pipe frame for a vine arbour, which had fallen down, and the few vines were mostly dead, but a vine arbour still seemed like a good idea. I mentally added a couple of large square pillars topped with heraldic beasts at the entrance and perhaps a row of brick pillars either side of the short drive to give the arbour a bit more gravitas; the metal framework could be adapted and set into the pillars to train the vines. The Spanish take their entrance gates seriously and usually build imposing pillars with hefty iron gates long before they start building a house.

With all these ideas swirling around, Antonio seemed a good man to ask about ploughing the weed-infested, goat-impacted patch of ground that was going to be our garden and orchard. José el Vino, the local contractor, used a monstrous Lamborghini tractor that was ideal for deep ploughing and stump pulling, but would barely have room to turn on our patch. Antonio agreed and mentioned that he would shortly be ploughing his potato patch.

'*No problema,*' he grinned. 'We will do it at the same time, don't worry.'

Returning from one of our interminable form-filling trips to obtain our *Residencia* permits there was a surprise: a pair of oxen was ploughing Antonio's patch. The huge, docile beasts were perfectly behaved, stopping and wheeling to voice commands as they effortlessly pulled the heavy iron plough, turning over the furrows as straight as any tractor. Unlike José's gigantic tractor, they couldn't deep plough, but neither did they compact the fragile sandy soil with their neatly trimmed and buffed black hooves.

With the ground prepared, we set off after Christmas to go to a *vivero* (garden centre) with a shopping list of trees. Almond, apricot, avocado, custard apple, grapefruit, kumquat, lemon, mandarin, orange, peach and pear. The very words conjured up a picture of us picking the luscious fruit off the trees, sun-warm juices dribbling down our chins.

It was just a pity that we would have to salivate for years before some of the trees reached maturity. Piling into the truck, we set off towards Alhaurin de la Torre on the Railway Road, so called because there had once been a railway link between Malaga and Alhaurin el Grande, which, having been axed by a Spanish Dr Beeching, had simply been filled in and tarmacked. Halfway there, an ominous grinding noise was shortly followed by a loud bang, an abrupt halt and dead silence. We got out with heavy hearts and James had a token look under the bonnet, but he knew at once what it was: the poor little Tonka was dead.

It was seriously bad news. We hadn't been planning to buy any other transport and although the Toyota was slow and small, it was also practical for hauling building materials. We were also many miles from home on a seemingly deserted road, so it was with huge relief that we saw a car pull up. The driver asked if he could tow us home and we gratefully accepted, but from then on the conversation went downhill.

'*Donde vive,*' where do you live?' he asked, quite reasonably.

James and I looked at each other in horror. 'Er, near La Cabra.'

'*Si,* but on which road?'

We searched memory banks, but it was no good, we just didn't know where our road went, and hadn't got the Spanish to explain that we were strangers around here.

'The road to La Cabra,' I repeated again.

'*Si, claro*, but WHICH road to La Cabra?'

There are many roads into La Cabra and our rescuer was obviously tiring of our circular conversation. When stressed my brain totally shuts down. Rudely regal, I pointed up the road down which we had travelled so hopefully. '*Anda,* go, I tell you when to stop.'

Half-an-hour later we arrived back at Finca Tara and thanked our bemused rescuer profusely – no wonder the Brits have a bad reputation as linguists and imperialists.

æ

'When the hounds of spring are on winter's traces,' yodelled Algernon Swinburne. Our hounds were a damp, smelly and windswept lot as February arrived in a flurry of gales and cloudbursts. The drought that had afflicted Andalucia for the past two years was over with a vengeance and now we began to see some unexpected defects in the house. As much water dripped down the internal walls as down the outside, and the newly whitewashed walls developed scabrous greeny-grey patches and a damp tidemark along the skirting that rose imperceptibly every day. The floors sweated and oozed, dew formed on every surface, and our clothes and shoes turned green. After one particularly hard and prolonged rainstorm, there was a small waterfall running down the dining hall wall that spread into a puddle, and then a flood that had to be constantly mopped to keep it under control. Grimly we built ever-larger fires in an effort to stay dry, much to the cats' delight, but bedding, clothes and towels were all damp and clammy.

Ulla hadn't been entirely frank with us. Although the roof looked to be in good condition, the old terracotta hand-made tiles were as porous as a sponge once they were thoroughly wet, so they would have to come off and a proper waterproof membrane fitted. This was another serious blow; another unforeseen expense that we had to find money for; another glitch to be dealt with before we could open for business.

There were compensations: in between the gales the sun shone warmly and spring flowers carpeted the land. The banks of the *río,* now a powerful and deep brook, were swathed in the indigo and glossy green of vinca, while the trees waded through drifts of golden trefoils, striated with tiny garnet and mauve orchids. Wild mint and sage mixed intriguingly with the piercingly-sweet scent of the orange blossom that lay like an aromatherapy blanket over the orchards. Antonio came over as I looked at our ratty old fruit trees, full of dead twigs and the shrivelled remains of last year's unpicked crop.

'*Sus árboles son muy feos,*' he announced bluntly. 'Your trees are useless and the wrong sort anyway: *chinas* (the original variety came from China, and were prized for their appearance and perfume rather than flavour) are tasteless, only good for juice, and the others are *bigarades,* bitter and not popular in the market.'

He was correct: I had just tried one and it was insipid and full of pips.

'There are many better varieties. Come, I will show you.' He walked over to his orchard that stood like a verdant island in the middle of our land. 'See these trees; these are good for juice and eating.' He handed me a heavy, medium-sized orange. 'Also you can have an orange *and* lemon tree such as this...' he pointed to a tree that had oranges on one side of it and lemons on the other.

'How on earth do you grow those?'

'Very simple. All these fruit trees are grafted onto wild root stock. Look, you can see the join here.' He pointed a grubby finger at a ridged piece at the bottom of the trunk. 'You can grow whatever you want on the one tree. Also you must have a lunar lemon tree, it never stops.' Antonio indicated a tree thick with blossom, studded with tiny unripe fruit the size of a thumbnail alongside large, ripe lemons. He pulled off enough for gallons of lemonade or 20 lemon meringue pies and stuffed them into a plastic bag produced from the depths of a pocket. 'Here you are, but see, first of all you must clean your trees.' A small tree-saw appeared from another pocket and he quickly trimmed off a few branches, 'Like this and this, so it's a good shape to pick the fruit and the air and sun can get in.'

'Do you get a good price for your citrus fruit Antonio? Has joining the EU helped?'

Antonio's stubbled face darkened. 'The price is bad, the worst ever. Now they're saying that we must not grow lemons anymore, that only Italy may grow lemons. *Pah*, we have always grown lemons, the best lemons. Why should *we* stop?'

Not having any answer to this, I thanked him for the fruit and walked back up to the house through the carpet of spring flowers, to find drifts of dwarf irises poking reticulated purple and gold buds like dragonfly wings through the newly laid gravel in front of the house.

James and I had been wondering about a cash crop on the land, but citrus was obviously not going to be the answer. Ulla had said she received a tiny income from the olives and oranges, and a bit more for the algarroba beans, as locals would come by and offer to pick them for half the profit. But as the soil was free-draining and the slope south-facing, I wondered if aloe vera might be the answer. Or perhaps ostriches? Or ducks?

We looked into the possibilities of each, but there seemed to be snags to everything. The aloe vera plants were expensive and the only refinery on the Costa del Sol was running at full capacity. The ostriches needed wire-fenced paddocks and could break your leg with a kick. Also, the Spanish are deeply conservative about their food and persuading them to eat exotic meat such as ostrich could be a problem. The ducks were an easier option, but they are so endearing I didn't think I could slaughter them. It was another impasse.

3.
Napoleon Lives!

Apil seemed just around the corner, considering how much there was to do before we could offer farmhouse holidays with any realistic hopes of clients enjoying themselves. The house as it stood was reasonably attractive but basic, consisting of three bedrooms opening onto a courtyard, a bathroom, a dining hall, and a sitting room with a fireplace in the corner and cripplingly uncomfortable concrete benches built into the walls.

The electricity had originally been installed by someone who was a *campesino* on Sunday and an electrician on Monday, at a time when a single power point in a room was considered ample. The only modern bit of wiring was for the three-phase electric pump that raised the water from our well on the bank of the *río*, up the steep incline through the olives and the elderly citrus trees to the storage tank on the roof via a complicated system of branching iron pipes and massive wheel valves. It looked like it could have been designed by Brunel, except that he would have made a better job of it. The water took an age to force its way through sclerotic pipework from the tank on the roof to the tiny gas heater in the kitchen, and from there to the bathroom, so that it was at best on the cool side of lukewarm. And when the gas cylinder ran out midway through, as it frequently did, it was the freezing side of cool. The third time I had to rinse my hair with a trickle of icy water was the moment I realised that guests might also find this a step too far on the back to nature trail.

Once the roof tank was full and the overflow was cascading down the rustic tiles with its burden of mozzie larvae, the water was diverted, with much tugging and heaving at the half-rusted valve wheels, to the garden *aljibe* (Arabic for water cistern). The pump was so powerful that if it was left on too long the overflow couldn't cope and the cement-domed top of the *aljibe* would start to lift and wobble in a frantic belly dance. Until I got around to creating a proper garden, the *aljibe* supplied water to a dustbowl, studded with weeds and olive trees, where our Teutonic neighbour Traudl chose to keep her goats, despite having more land than we did. This was not a difficulty in itself, but the goats had been tethered there for so long that they had impacted the ground and stripped the trees, but she saw no reason to move them. A courteous request to move the animals because we wanted to plough the ground got a negative response.

'But zey are happy, und zey alvays live zere.' She turned and walked away, the matter settled.

'But...Traudl, this is going to be our garden,' I bleated, trotting after her, '...really, it would be better if you moved them to your land. Look, you have a shady patch similar to this.'

'Nein,' the corn-coloured plaits swung vigorously, 'ven I make zat a garden, ze goats zey voud eat ze plants.'

There was no easy reply to this and as it seemed a bit early in our relationship with the Rhine maiden to point out that it was her problem not ours, I left it for the moment. Traudl had an American live-in boyfriend, an electronics engineer called Chuck who was a lot easier to get on with than her, and he often dropped in for a coffee and a chat, or to offer help with building problems. James was happy to talk things through with him as Chuck knew a bit about building and electrical matters, so when he offered to help with the swimming pool we accepted gratefully.

Diego turned up unannounced early one morning with an architect in tow, hammering on the bedroom window until we awoke. It had been a night hideous with feline yowling and shrieking as Antonio's pride created the next generation, and we clambered out of bed bleary-eyed and woolly-headed to let them in and to make coffee. In the sitting room I found Luigi cowering under the sofa. His terror at hearing his tormentor the ginger tom had caused him to lose control of his bowels, several times, on the cream Indian shagpile carpet.

Amazingly, in the space of an hour, we thrashed out what we wanted to do with the house and pool. The architect had some good ideas, which seemed expensive at £1,000 for his fee, but Diego said that was the going rate to get the permissions from the College of Architects, and we could save lots of money by calling the pool an *aljibe*. This was quite normal practice in this part of Andalucia – sensible even – as there were frequent bush fires in summer and the *bomberos* could help themselves to your pool on their way to a blaze.

We decided to add two bathrooms and a kitchenette which, after a few internal changes, would give us a self-contained apartment with either one or two bedrooms – depending on which doors were locked – plus a further large bedroom with en-suite in the main building, and a fourth bedroom in what had once been the garage.

Ten years previously, Ulla had made the dreadful error of building the garage three inches the wrong side of the boundary with our other neighbour *El Rata* (the Rat). Spanish *campesinos* take the matter of boundaries very seriously indeed, despite the practical difficulties of defining them. Any enquiry as to where a property's boundary might be in this almost fenceless land will elicit an airy wave of the hand at a stone, a tree or a ditch. What happens if the stone is moved, the tree is cut down or the ditch filled? Well, just ask an old man – virtually any handy, elderly *campesino* will do. They have amazing memories for the minutiae of the land because over a certain age they're virtually all illiterate. They will tell you not only where the boundary is, but also who moved the stone, who chopped the tree down and which storm filled the ditch. I dare say a total stranger to the area could also provide this service: he would pick up on the patch cultivated differently, the superior pruning of one orchard over its neighbour, mule ploughed ground next to ox ploughed, the greener crop or the leaner goats. To us, it is just countryside; to them, it is sacred, *el campo dorado* (the golden land). Their plot receives the loving attention normally accorded a new wife or mistress in northern Europe, and if nature and circumstances frown on their efforts, they will wrestle with the land through a life of poverty until death is the promise and the reward.

Neighbours have blood feuds lasting generations rather than give up a *pulga* (an inch, literally a thumb) of their precious land.

Ulla, being northern European *and* a woman, didn't quite get this, despite having a good command of Spanish, so when the Rat told her she couldn't build her garage on his boundary, or use his track to get onto the *acequia* road, she briskly told him not to be a silly little man as he had lots of land, or words to that effect. The next time she took a trip to America on business she returned to find *El Rata* had built a brick wall the length of their joint boundary, a five-foot wall that sealed off her garage and car from the outside world.

Ulla conceded defeat, so he dismantled enough of the wall for her to remove her car and then carefully rebuilt the wall, ensuring that Ulla would never again use the garage for its intended purpose.

'You look out for *El Rata,* he's a thoroughly nasty bit of work,' she warned us ruefully.

With this warning in mind, we waited in some trepidation for the hard man of the *campo* to visit the olive shed he had built just feet away from the side of our house, although his land stretched over the horizon; a not very subtle reminder to Ulla of the garage war. One morning I was painting the side of the house when the put-put of a moto heralded his arrival. Peering through the skip-course brickwork of *El Rata*'s revenge, I saw a tiny old man with a pitted walnut face and the soggy remains of a cigarette stuck to the side of his mouth, under a sweat-stained organic green trilby that must have seen at least 50 years of service. The moto pillion was piled higher than his head with a ziggurat of plastic crates roped together into a tottering pile which had miraculously survived our pot-holed track. Forgetting he couldn't see me in the gloom between wall and house I brightly chirped a greeting.

'*Buenos días, Señor... er...*' I thought better of calling him by his nickname.

¡'Ha! *Quien es,* who is it?' he demanded suspiciously, looking searchingly into a bramble bush. Observing his profile it was easy to see how he had come by his nickname.

'*Sus vecinos nuevos,*' I said, sticking my neighbourly paint-splodged hand through the wall.

'*Madre Dios, los Inglés,*' he muttered disgustedly, looking around furtively before grasping my fingers gingerly by the tips and waggling them. News travelled fast here.

As the permissions were in the pipeline we needed to get on with the building work as fast as possible, and for that we needed a crew. Chuck recommended going to Cristóbal's bar on the railway road, situated in what was once the station siding, and discussing in a loud voice, in Spanish of course, what needed to be done.

This wasn't easy on several counts: the entrance to the bar was guarded by a surly dog leashed to a running tackle on a cable that stretched across the entrance. Any move to enter the bar caused the mangy beast to hurtle to and fro as if on rails, yelping frantically, thereby warning the natives that a stranger was about to invade their territory. The noise in the bar made Juan's place sound like the Reading Room of the British Museum, as a bunch of *peones* (workers hired by the day) enjoyed a heated argument about football. The level of embarrassment suffered in Juan's Bar on Christmas Day paled into insignificance against the nightmare of having to make ourselves heard in village-idiot level Spanish over the shouts of the well-oiled clientele, the blare of the TV, and the incessant barking of the dog as swarthy men came in to buy chicken wire and tyre sandals, nails and mattocks and all manner of rural goodies, this being a hardware store as well as a bar. They all looked aghast at me, and my embarrassment was increased on realising that it was a 'men only' bar. Despite all this, the plan worked like magic: there was a knock on our door a couple of hours later and foreman Antonio Manuel, *el jefe,* announced that he had come to help us.

As my Spanish was slightly more advanced than James's, I attempted to explain to Antonio Manuel what we needed doing, soon realising we had a problem: a certain type of Iberian male doesn't take technical instructions from a woman. He would only talk to James and totally ignored me. This cultural impasse was overcome by my standing behind James and talking in a gruff voice like a third-class ventriloquist act, but it was enough to salve Antonio Manuel's male pride and we soon agreed on terms.

The next morning he turned up with his sidekick José who was a goatherd when he wasn't being a builder, and Paco, who sold ladies' knickers in the evenings. Paco had the strange habit of squatting on the roof singing *cante hondo* (emotional, flamenco gypsy music) like a bipolar vampire bat when he was having a bad knickers week, and he had to be gently talked down, whereupon he would follow us into the house to give us his views on life and the human situation. James was unblocking the toilet yet again when Paco wandered in on this occasion. Looking gravely at his employer with his head down the bowl, he announced in a lugubrious voice, '*Amigos*, shit and death are the same for all men.' This was so profound that we had to have several beers to ponder Paco's philosophical insights.

To our crew, all *guiris* (foreigners) were rich beyond the dreams of avarice. They couldn't and wouldn't believe that we were poor compared with most expats, but as long as their wages were paid in cash every Friday they weren't too worried. The myth of the lazy Spanish worker soon evaporated as we tried to keep pace with our crew, who turned up at 7.30 every morning on mopeds hung with buckets and trowels. Setting fire to any of our personal possessions left lying around, they stood shivering in the mountain air for the time it took to smoke a vile-smelling, hand-rolled ciggie, followed by bouts of lung-wracking coughing. They worked until five, with brief breaks for breakfast and lunch, both of which were taken at Juan's Bar and seemed to consist of coffee, brandy and a smoke. Unlike their British counterparts, they never drank tea (they did try it one particularly cold day when I insisted they have a hot drink, but the general consensus was that it smelt and tasted like sick goat's pee), and scorned our instant coffee. Spain is classless when it comes to food and drink, with the result that you can get an excellent cup of real coffee throughout the country irrespective of whether it's the Ritz in Madrid or Cristóbal's bar; the only, and very considerable difference being the price.

Although the men worked like demons they needed watching on the 20th century details. The normal way of installing a toilet at that time in a Spanish *campo* house was to bung it down anywhere handy in the bathroom and remove the waste via an open concrete gulley to the *pozo negro*, a type of cesspit. Therefore when James announced that we were installing plastic plumbing and described the technological delights of swept bends and rodding-eyes, they were a bit dubious, obviously feeling this new-fangled nonsense wouldn't catch on. Luckily we caught *el jefe* customising his own perceived version of a swept bend out of a piece of guttering with the aid of a blowtorch, before it was buried out of sight under the floor tiles.

There were many interior changes to be made: walls to be removed or added with new windows and doors, but altering your house in this way isn't a problem in Spain as interior walls generally aren't load-bearing, so there's no need for RSJs or lintels. We loved the Moorish arches you see everywhere in Andalucia, so whenever possible we made archways rather than doors. It's possible to buy arch formers off the shelf, but Antonio Manuel scorned this sort of prissy conservatism and was as keen as we were to keep costs down. Taking lengths of reinforcing rod, he bent them to shape as easily as if they'd been wire coat hangers, followed by a skin of plywood. When it was all plastered up, the arches were perfect, both in proportion and shape, echoing the arched shelves built into the walls.

The bathroom door didn't close properly, offering an instant view to anyone coming through the front door of the brown toilet and any occupant, so it had to go. We asked Antonio Manuel to open a new doorway in a different wall and to brick up the old one, and, impressed with his artistic sense, we asked him to form a small recess in the brickwork for a lovely old plaster Madonna that we'd found at Fuengirola fleamarket. At this point we had to make one of our lengthy and frustrating visits to Eduardo the *abogado*, solicitors being possibly even worse (and certainly slower) in Andalucia than anywhere else in the civilised world. It was late when we returned and the men had left. The house was in darkness as James opened the front door and switched on the light. I bumped into his back as he recoiled in horror.

'What the hell is *that*?' he screeched.

Facing us, in place of the old bathroom door, was what appeared to be a brick built Mayan sacrificial altar. Seven foot tall and proportionately broad, it imbued the whole room with a sepulchral gloom, the sacrificial aspect heightened by Luigi lying stretched out asleep on top of it.

It was tricky next day telling Antonio Manuel that it would have to go.

'*Esta es magnifico Señora*, your niche for the Madonna,' he said, glowing with pride.

'Um, *si, ciertamente Antonio Manuel, pero no está exactamente...*' I stumbled miserably, 'perhaps it's a bit bigger than I imagined.' I was beginning to think James had it sussed, pretending he couldn't speak Spanish. It was all too obvious that one of us should be taking lessons, and I knew who would be voted to carry the linguistic can.

↬

By this time the brochures had been designed and printed and were ready to be sent out, but the pool was still a hole in the ground. José el Vino's JCB teetered on the steep bank for a day scraping out the basic shape, cutting away the earth until three sides were cut into the slope, with one long wall exposed. James, Chuck and I laid the footings in a five-hour marathon on a scorching February day, the temperature hitting 120°F in the south-facing pit. The local blacksmith constructed the reinforcing mesh for the floor and walls and, as money was tight, we scoured the countryside for timber, planks and corrugated iron sheets for the shuttering and cut some of our diseased old trees for piling. When the whole 'Mad Max' edifice was complete, the ready-mixed concrete truck arrived and the great pour began. *El jefe* stood below the pool, his jaw white with tension as he eyed the shuttering on the exposed long wall. The rest of us were more cautious and stood up-slope as the cement cascaded down the chute from the lorry. Three loads later it was finished and the cement lorry trundled off to sighs of relief ...which quickly turned to cries of horror as a section of the shuttering gave way and cement poured down the hill in a bubbling lava torrent. James and I looked at each other in despair. The tears ran down my face as I turned to go into the house, and Paco and José looked like they would like to go home too, but Antonio Manuel was made of sterner stuff. His dark face mottled with fury as he transmogrified into a strutting pint-sized tyrant, haranguing us until we were white-lipped and shaking.

'*Hombres, dar la vuelta a trabajar inmediamente...*' he snarled, 'get back to work.'

Cowed, we did just that and with frenzied speed two of us got the cement mixer going, making up a stiff mix with lots of curing agent so it would go off fast, while the others tore the planking off Antonio's goat shed and banged it over the gap. We poured and poured and poured again, as night fell and bats swooped around our heads to the accompaniment of the outraged bleating of homeless goats and a shed-less neighbour.

James and I were up at dawn the next day, sick with anxiety... but it was perfect, you couldn't even see the join. The pool is still in use, a monument to ignorance, incompetence and our tyrant *jefe* who simply refused to lose face. Funnily enough, Antonio Manuel's family had originally come from Corsica and just for a moment there in the dusk, he reminded me strongly of a certain gentleman called Bonaparte.

⮞

We noticed after a while that the cat population over the road rose and fell quite alarmingly, taking into consideration that passing traffic wasn't fast enough for road kill, and we reluctantly concluded that Antonio reared them as livestock. In the bad old days after the Civil War when there was little food, there was a tradition in Andalucia for the plump 'fiesta cat', which I'm reliably informed tastes like rabbit. Possibly that's why the head is always left on the carcass of rabbits offered for sale in local butchers' shops and supermarkets?

My bad thoughts about neighbour Antonio and the cats were reinforced shortly afterwards. The men were laying a cement bed for the terracotta tiles around the pool and had just finished smoothing and levelling when Smoo, in that infuriating way cats have, deliberately strolled through it. I could see Paco muttering furiously and the others were disgruntled, so I picked up a pebble and chucked it in his general direction to scare him off. The men joined in with a will with rather larger and more accurate stones, so thinking it best to remove him before he got hurt, I walked off around the side of the house calling him after me.

I settled down to do some more house painting and half an hour or so later saw Smoo swaggering up the track from the land with a fine rabbit in his mouth. 'Goody,' I thought, 'we can have some of that for supper and the cats can have the rest.' Taking it off him I skinned and gutted it, and removed the head and feet, giving Smoo some offal as a reward. While he wolfed down the goodies, I walked back around the house to get to the kitchen, giving the men a sweet forgiving smile as I passed; I knew they hadn't really meant to hurt Smoo, merely to steer him away with pebbles as they would a goat. But the three of them stood transfixed: silent, shocked eyes swivelling from the rabbit to the large bloody jack-knife in my other hand.

It was a bit puzzling. Why would they be upset about a rabbit, one of their favourite meats? It was a good hour later that I realised their illusions about the pet-loving British had been shattered. A skinned rabbit without the head and feet looks exactly the same as a skinned cat – and the bloody jack-knife in my hand proved I was capable of a country woman's casual acceptance that animals are for the pot.

'*¡Mira el gato!*' Look, the cat! Shouts of laughter and clapping announced the arrival of Smoo, the Imperial Rabbit, and I went out to explain that while the English may eat their livestock, they never, but never, eat their pet cats!

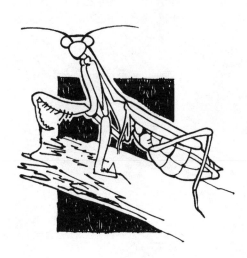

4.
The Water Fairy

The pool seemed to have made up its mind to stay in one place and was left to cure and harden for a few weeks. It was time to landscape around it and make a lawn for the guests to loll on. Ulla had introduced us to José el Vino as someone who could help us in many practical ways as he had a wealth of agricultural tools and an extended family skilled in every aspect of horticulture. He also had an electrician son who could issue *boletins* (an official report on an electrical installation stating that it is up to the standard required), a useful contact for James as major electrical work had to be signed off by a state-qualified electrician.

We put on our calling clothes. Icy dewdrops sparkled on the cobwebs as we walked up the lane in the thin, chilly sunshine, and we were shivering as Mrs José welcomed us into a room distinguished – but not in any way brightened or cheered – by the quantity of religious iconography that hung on every wall. Anyone with a convent education will recognise the thrill of guilt associated with the bleeding heart of Jesus. In the middle of the room was a round table covered with a thick felt cloth, at which sat an old lady, introduced as José's mother.

Mrs J sat us down and it was a delicious surprise to find it was toasty-warm under the tablecloth, heated by a *brasero* of charcoal embers built into the base of the table. James and I luxuriated as our frozen toes came to life and Mrs J bustled around making coffee in an old black saucepan. As we talked to José about our garden needs, an ancient rusty-black cat ambled in and wriggled under the tablecloth.

José had a cousin who worked as a gardener on one of the big urbanisations on the coast who would certainly give us a hand, which would be extremely helpful as I had no idea what type of grass to plant or what would grow well.

José was now well into his stride and determined we should try his wine. 'I am the best wine maker in the village,' he announced with a total lack of humility. 'This is why I'm called *José del Vino*, José of the Wine.' He went out to a shed and returned with a carboy of dark, viscous liquid, which he sloshed into large tumblers. 'This is my vintage of last year, it's very good, lots of plum and strawberry notes, try it.'

We sipped and made appreciative noises. It was vile beyond belief – sickeningly sweet, cloying and about 16 per cent proof. James was knocking his back in great swigs and had started to giggle – a bad sign. I finished my tumbler with relief and took a gulp of coffee to wash away the foul taste. A feeble croak forced its way past my clenched teeth as the coffee hit my stomach. Mrs J must have learned her coffee-making technique in the souks of Istanbul.

'*Venga,* come on, we've hardly started, there are other wines to try, my sweet dessert wine is especially notorious.' José brandished another carboy and a bottle with a hand-printed label in our horrified faces. However, there are times when courtesy is more important than health, common-sense or personal taste. James and I looked at each other meaningfully and gritted our rapidly blackening teeth. By the third glass, James was fingering his nose. This was the worst sign of all, as it meant his nose had gone numb and he was pretty well off his face. I was feeling wobbly too. The sweet dessert wine had a kick like an army mule and my tongue seemed to be swelling; at any rate it was becoming difficult to talk.

José wanted to demonstrate his new TV, which was so large it wouldn't have looked out of place in a Premiership footballer's pad, and they had been forced to put it against the far wall in the bedroom next door in order to sit far enough away to watch it. We all leaned our heads together and peered through the doorway to watch this miracle of technology, but the signal was so weak it resembled one of those 'snowstorm in a bottle' things on a grandiose scale. Every time we tried to leave, José held up a finger. 'Wait, you *must* see this,' he said, as yet another amply-bosomed fuzzy Señora howled about the life-threatening properties of love.

I was despairing of ever getting away when I noticed a thin

wisp of what appeared to be smoke curling up from James's lap, but he seemed unaware of it and was giggling happily. The smoke thickened by the second, accompanied by an unpleasant whiff of scorching hair.

'Tzzzzzt... James, *James!*' I hissed.

Abruptly everybody sat upright and stared at James, who gazed back through the billowing cloud. He had now stopped giggling and was looking worried and fumbling surreptitiously at his flies, clearly perplexed by the etiquette involved in finding his crotch on fire in the presence of elderly and devout ladies.

Gran clacked her dentures in irritation at having her viewing interrupted, and with what sounded suspiciously like a muttered oath, twitched back the tablecloth to reveal the ancient cat lying on James's lap with its tail on fire. Grasping her coffee cup she hurled its contents between my husband's legs with a deft and practised movement. There was a splutter and the cat jumped down and stalked off angrily, lashing its sodden and still slightly smoking tail. This seemed like a good time to say our farewells and we staggered home coffee-stained, drugged to the eyeballs with caffeine and stomachs roiling with enough high-proof alcohol to incinerate a thousand Christmas puddings.

José was as good as his word and his cousin Pepe turned up in his Mercedes van the next day to find out what we wanted. He was keen to show me the gardens where he worked, so that I could pick out the flowers and plants I wanted, and we set out down the long winding road to the coast. It didn't take long to realise two things; Pepe wore an after-shave so strong it brought tears to my eyes and he had pretensions to be a racing driver. Before we were halfway down I was gasping with terror and olfactory overload, but my pleas to go a bit slower merely meant he took his hands off the wheel to point out how well the van handled at speed on the tight corners.

The gardens were well worth seeing, a riot of geranium, bougainvillea, jasmine, hibiscus and datura. He explained that the grass, unlike our English lawn grass, isn't seeded but propagated by stolons, little pieces of grass that rapidly form rootlets. He would literally bring the lawn to us in sacks, sprigs picked by hand from the grama grass lawns in his gardens. As we walked around the immaculate grounds he told me the most important thing about establishing a garden was water, lots and lots of water.

'*Agua, necesite mucha, mucha agua,*' he would repeat every few minutes.

When he turned up a few days later with 20 sacks of grama grass, some goat-pellet fertiliser and his tools to plant the lawn, I got a further instalment of '*Mucha, mucha agua,*' as he obviously suspected I hadn't grasped it the first time. Pepe was very large indeed, with long hairy arms like a gorilla's and a hairline perched half an inch above his nose, but he was also sweet-natured, so he was named The Water Fairy.

Over the next few weeks the cry of '*Agua, mucha, mucha agua*' heralded the frequent visits of The Water Fairy with plants and trees, quite a few of which I'm sure he'd 'borrowed' from his place of work. The grass sprigs, which had been planted in perfect rows, one stolon to a square inch, took amazingly fast: within a month there was a lawn with trees and a flower bed edging the pool. I'd been diligent and lavished water on the lawn, pumping up twice a day so I could drizzle and drench the precious cuttings, ignoring the electricity meter whizzing around as the three-phase pump pushed the water up the hill – even so, The Water Fairy's brow furrowed with disappointment every time he visited.

'*Agua, necesite mucha, mucha agua,*' he said, shaking his shaggy head over my inability to grasp the simplest gardening truths. In fact it had only just struck me that our soil was so poor and free-draining that it must be almost pure sand. Antonio nodded his agreement when I asked him.

'*Claro que si,* your land is very poor.' He pointed at his vegetable patch. 'I also have a piece here that is bad. I have to put much manure on it to grow anything.'

I nodded and felt slightly queasy. We had been enjoying the fresh-picked vegetables our kindly neighbour often brought over. James and I had laughed about Antonio's dawn 'mooning' behind olive trees on his veggie patch. We knew he didn't have indoor sanitation, but hadn't thought beyond that. I now realised that peasant farmers waste nothing – the joke was on us.

Work wasn't going quite so well indoors, as we couldn't afford pre-mixed paint and the *cal* (a lime paint like distemper) has to be mixed by hand in a vat using lumps of lime, water and colorant. It hisses and fizzes as it's mixed and heats up quite alarmingly, as well as burning your skin, but gives a nice soft finish appropriate to a country house. But, every batch turns out a different colour as it isn't an exact science, so if you don't mix enough you have to give it yet another coat. I wanted to complete the bedrooms as we were looking forward to our first visitors. Keef and Becky both had practical and inventive minds and we still had a few problems to solve, such as how to build a concrete table to seat ten in the garden.

&

We had begun to meet a few of the expats who lived in the neighbourhood. People were friendly and would introduce themselves in the village shop, the front room of a small house wedged between a bar and a small hall, where village activities such as Sevillana dance classes took place, or in Juan's bar. The acknowledged lord and lady of the manor, Jack and Maud, had retired from Norfolk to a large and comfortable house in its own grounds on the edge of the village. They took their duties seriously in the nicest possible way, and as soon as they were aware of our presence, they made a social call to ask us to a barbie. La Esperanza (The Hope) was an eye-opener. The modern two-storey house stood in the centre of its estate, surrounded by a plantation of manicured mandarin trees in perfectly regimented lines. The earth under the trees was harrowed free of weeds, the long drive was sentried with palms and sparkled with freshly-raked white marble chippings.

Everything was trimmed, burnished, mown, swept and immaculate.

What a contrast with Finca Tara. Our poor, old untended citrus and olive trees straggled down the slope to the river, ragged with dead twigs, fruits small and hard with the unequal struggle against rampant grasses and lack of water. Antonio's little *huerta* that pushed a pseudopod into our land showed what our plot could look like with a great deal of work. The boundary between us was clearly marked by tilled earth and vigorous shapely trees dripping with fruit. Even his olive trees looked different, with all the suckers cleared from the trunks and the branches pruned to a low-spreading shape to make the harvest easier. James was aching to get onto the land to prune the trees and tidy it all up a bit. Seeing our neighbours' trees made him green with envy, but other things had a higher priority.

☙

A call to the removers in England alerted us that our furniture was on the way and John and Dennis turned up the next morning. John's rich mahogany tan hinted that they might have stopped here and there, but after unpacking there was only one slightly damaged chair to grumble about. As it was late, we invited them to stay the night and took them for a meal in Alhaurin el Grande. For some reason, everything was closed except for a tiny hotel in the centre of town that we had barely noticed before, where the menu though short was extremely reasonable. The boys said they weren't too keen on continental food and wanted fish and chips, so we ordered the nearest thing to it, *fritura Malagueña* and fries. John and Dennis painstakingly sorted out the mouth-wateringly crisp and tasty little squid and whitebait in their feather-light batter and swept them to one side, grumbling that they only liked the cod. I silently wondered how a nation surrounded by some of the best fish in the world came to embrace fish-fingers and something nameless in a straitjacket of sticky, fatty dough.

It was quite late now and as we sat over our coffee catching up on the news from our part of Somerset (we had used a local removal firm), I realised that quite a few men had come in, had a meal or a drink and then gone upstairs, followed by one or other of the waitresses. After ten minutes or so the waitress would come down again, followed by the man. Then another man would go upstairs with another waitress. The traffic up and down the stairs seemed heavy for such a small hotel, and I wondered why the waitresses needed to go up as well. Did they have to make up the beds in the absence of chambermaids? A tiny suspicion grew, but the others didn't seem to notice anything and although one hears of champagne being drunk out of ladies' shoes, and even services being rendered in exchange for lunch vouchers, I had never heard of a brothel providing an excellent value fish supper. The Spanish are pragmatic though and the only other 'establishment' in town that we knew of was a tiny cabin with a simple traffic light system: red for no and green for go. The only drawback was that the parking space was bang on the main road, so a distinctive car could be a disadvantage.

At this time Malaga airport had two arrival halls at different ends of the building and anything up to 12 flights an hour arriving. Keef and Becky had found a cheap flight, but hadn't been able to give us a flight number, so James went down at about the right time and ran from one hall to the other until they appeared. This was going to be a problem with our guests, as Telefonica had stated that they couldn't give us a phone line for at least four years and had no plans to enlarge the local exchange. They are a government monopoly, so threats and entreaties don't concern them. For the moment we would have to manage with the phone in Juan's bar and our agent in England who would take the bookings. Jack and Maud had offered to take any emergency calls from our families and we couldn't ask them to do any more.

When they arrived, Keef and Becky set to with a will and

with their help we moved mountains. Keef is an engineer with a decided talent for wacky inventions and he had no difficulty designing a cost-free, non-electrical method of measuring the water level in the new *deposito,* a separate chamber built onto the swimming pool structure to replace the asbestos roof tank. This was quite important, as overfilling the *deposito* was wasteful, and letting it run dry involved lifting a cripplingly-heavy manhole cover and fiddling around with spanners and a watering can priming the system again. When we had guests, we got through a couple of tankfulls every day, and they were always highly amused to see the red-flagged wand rising mysteriously out of the terracotta paving like an Indian rope trick.

Our guests also built a palatial garden shed for me to hide in and cracked the problem of the concrete table for ten, which was cast in situ. Getting the massive table top onto its pedestal required the help of every able-bodied person within a mile, but it looked great, and was set off by the marble-topped benches around it. I'd seen these cheap pieces of marble in our local *mármol* yard, the off-cuts that result from cutting out the basin shape from a bathroom unit, and they'd been lying around for months – a solution looking for a problem.

The deceased Acty truck was converted into a trailer and most of the dead trees were cut and stacked for firewood. Suddenly the place was looking a bit more respectable, although a visit to La Esperanza put things into perspective. We had done a lot, but there was much still to do before the paying punters arrived and no money to do it. The cash put aside for renovation was gone and it was a close run thing whether we would have enough in the bank to pay the men for their last week's work.

೨

Bedrooms can be amazingly uncomfortable, their drawbacks ranging from lack of reading lights to lumpy mattresses with too little or too much bedding. Having read that it's a good idea to spend the occasional night in the spare room to check it out, I did my best. However, it's a bit tricky when you simply don't have enough of anything and the furnishings had to be moved from room to room depending on the needs of the guests. There were 13 non-paying guests to practise on in the next few weeks in our roles of butler, chambermaid, chauffeur and chef.

Our readiness was put to the test the day a Belgian friend appeared out of the blue. Hortense had been touring Spain with an old companion, a dear man who just happened to be a Viscount and, should a certain country cease to be a republic, a pretender to its throne. They both had exquisite manners and comparatively simple tastes except, it has to be said, when it came to food and wine. Luckily they had brought some excellent bottles of wine with them, and I managed to cobble together meals for the couple of days they stayed.

Nothing seemed to work while they were there: the loo in their new bathroom refused to flush so, much to Hortense's embarrassment, she had to call for 'the plumber', who was also highly embarrassed as he rather fancied her. His insomniac lordship crashed around his room all night with frightful oaths, trying to find the light switches which were, admittedly, in strange places, one being inside the built-in wardrobe and the other behind a door. The bedside lamp, which was one of Ulla's American rejects, worked by turning a knob, or not, as the whim took it. Our well-heeled guests appeared to enjoy themselves despite everything, but as sometimes happens with friends who one doesn't know really well, the subject of money couldn't be broached. I'm sure they would have been horrified to know that the food they had eaten represented the very last of our cash, and we were too amateurish and socially inept to present them with a bill.

It was already the beginning of May; we were officially open for business and although our English agent had received 16 enquiries, there were no firm bookings and it was now crunch time. If there were no bookings before the end of May we might have to think again or even sell Finca Tara. We both developed colds and pimples as the full seriousness of the situation sank in. At the same time it was almost exciting to realise that unless we lived on our wits we would actually go hungry, something that just didn't happen in Britain to people like us. I was reading Karen Blixen's wonderful *Out of Africa*; her courage in keeping her coffee farm going when she had no money and no prospects was so inspirational I knew we couldn't just give in and we had to give it a chance. James, who always just got on with things in his own quiet way, was also depressed, but he started looking for work at Malaga airport as he was a highly-trained aeronautical engineer. There was nothing; in fact there was very little work available anywhere. I'm not sure which of us was more horrified when he returned home one afternoon as a Barratt timeshare tout. For shy, gentle James it was hell on earth. He stuck it out for a month being secretly coached by John, a face from the smoke who could sell pork luncheon-meat to a rabbinical canteen. One lunchtime they decided to chuck it in, as even John wasn't making more than petrol money, so they had a beer, then another beer and so on until they fell into some bushes and noisily passed out, finally being ejected by the security guard.

It was now my move and we needed cash fast, so some of our nicer pieces of furniture and pictures were sold to antique shops down on the coast, and we could eat again for a while.

Luigi was always trying to help out by eating any wildlife that came his way and often one would awake from a deep sleep to hyena-like crunching and slurping from beneath the bed as he hoovered up moths and beetles, mice and worms. The earthworms were frighteningly large, more like little snakes, and the poor birds struggled to get them out of the ground, leaning backwards and tugging with grim determination. All for nought, because as soon as the worm was above ground Luigi would stroll over, frighten the rightful owner off and spear the writhing worm with a claw while he sucked on it like a liquorice bootlace. Unfortunately it went to his head and one day he started to munch on a *really* big worm, which turned out to be a snake with a healthy desire not to be eaten. It wasn't poisonous, but it bit Luigi on the backside so thoroughly that for a while it was touch and go as the wound turned septic. Smoo looked after him, licking and no doubt admonishing him; luckily Smoo was far too sensible to get involved with anything but rabbits.

The relationship with Traudl remained difficult. For some reason she was convinced that her house was dusty because we drove past it too fast, and however slowly we went a note would appear under the front door demanding yet another apology. Finally she sent James a note that upset him deeply, although he wouldn't tell me what it was about. We would have preferred to be good neighbours but it seemed easier just to avoid her and her arguments. Despite our arms-length relationship she banged on the door one morning.

'Mrs James, voud you make sure my goat is alright, I zink she might have her baby und I must go schopping.'

No sooner had the dust from her departing car settled than the goat, which was still resident in our garden, started making piteous sounds and it was obvious the birth had started. The elderly mother had a bag hanging nearly to the ground and long untrimmed hooves that curled up at the ends like Turkish slippers. Luckily she needed the minimum of help, as despite being a farmer's daughter I'm no expert on birthing goats. After a rubdown the kid was standing within ten minutes of being born, but I couldn't get it suckling; it wasn't in the slightest bit interested and the mother wasn't helping at all, swinging away and kicking at it if it made a move towards her, although she must have been uncomfortably bursting with milk – this wasn't looking good. For the moment there was nothing more I could do, so I gave the nanny water and left them together in the shade hoping nature would take over. An hour later I went out to check on them and nearly fainted with horror. The nanny goat was pouring blood from several terrible deep slashes on her bag and it looked as though she had been attacked with a knife. Traudl's car was coming down the lane and I didn't know what to say to her.

'Mrs James, vot haf you done? Mein goat is bleeding, you haf ripped her?' Traudl's leading sally was just the start of it. I wanted her to get the vet, but apparently that would cost too much, which I could sympathise with, but then Traudl had an idea.

'I vill get Antonia. She vas alvays keeping goats. She vill know vot to do.'

This sounded like an excellent plan. Antonia lived at the top of our lane and would sometimes walk down to have a chat when her arthritis was up to it. She was ancient, with a kind face seamed and seared by sun and a hard life, making her look even older than her 88 years. She had lived through the terrible years of the Spanish Civil War as a nurse and wouldn't be upset by a little blood; she had seen everything that could be done to flesh.

'*Aah, la pobrecita,*' Antonia wheezed, 'She has cut herself. Look at those hooves, like razors! We must sew her up at once or the kid cannot drink.' She looked around. '*Venga*, bring the kitchen table out here, and we'll need another strong pair of hands, a good big needle and some strong thread.'

James was pressed into service and we swung the protesting goat onto the kitchen table as Antonia went to work, first sterilising the needle and thread, and then the goat's bag with some vodka I'd unearthed, then bending to her mending with her dim old eyes inches from the lacerations. We rethreaded the needle for her until all the tears were neatly sutured. Before the goat was allowed off the table I grabbed the pruning secateurs and lopped off the long sharp overgrowth of hoof that had caused the damage. The old goat seemed quite calm now and her one sound quarter was milked out into a baby's bottle so the kid could have a drink. By the next morning all was well: the bag was healing rapidly without a hint of infection and after 48 hours the kid was feeding normally. Peace had returned to our garden.

Traudl was so grateful that she now became as friendly as she had previously been hostile, and took to calling in several times a day, usually at the most awkward moments, to tell us about her life. The little Ulla had told us about Traudle's marriage turned out to be true. Her husband had been a Prussian sadist of the worst kind, and she had obviously had a sad and loveless life. This emotional baggage didn't make her present relationship with Chuck any easier; he admitted she could be difficult. Just how difficult we were about to discover.

5.
Caterpillar Wars

The pounding on the front door grew louder and more insistent as we tried to ignore it; we burrowed back under warm bedclothes seeking blessed sleep, hoping the noise would go away. But of course it didn't and finally we put on dressing gowns and opened the door.

Traudl stood there in her nightie and robe, red-eyed in the insect swarming lamplight.

'Chuck he shout, he hit me, he vant to stab me!' Pushing past into the sitting room she threw herself down on a sofa and examined a minute scratch on her hand. 'I must to stay here, he haf a knife from ze kitchen.'

She was very upset so we let her talk herself out, going over and over what had been said and done by Chuck, and what had been said and done in the past by her deceased husband Gerhard: it was a long night. James went over to have a word with Chuck and reported back that the knife had been put away – Chuck was sorry, it had all been a silly mistake, maybe a bad dream. Traudl seemed calmer after some tea and James and I were desperate for sleep after hours of male shortcomings, so she was persuaded to go home. We were asleep in seconds.

Screeching and a fusillade on the front door awakened us for the second time, a glance at the clock relaying the highly unwelcome information that it was 4.17am. It was with a certain amount of unneighbourly sighing that the door was opened to Traudl, once again in floods of tears.

'Chuck haf an udder knife, he vont to slice me. He say I keel my 'usband Gerhard and he vont to keel me before I keel heem.' Her voice was rising up the scale towards hysteria.

James and I looked at each other in concern. Although she was a big strapping girl who was a good head taller than Chuck, Traudl was genuinely frightened. One thing seemed odd: Chuck was normally such a quiet decent guy, not at all your run-of-the-mill axe murderer.

'James, I'm going over there to talk to Chuck,' I said. 'There could be something wrong. How did he seem to you?'

'Well, he was a bit rambling and confused now you come to mention it ... be careful.'

'He vill slice you Mrs James. He vill keel you. He is a murderer, call ze policia,' screeched Traudl.

She was starting to do my head in. Although I felt sorry for her, my strongest sympathies were with Chuck, who had a fair bit to cope with on a daily basis.

It came as a distinct relief to find Chuck was delirious with a raging fever of 101 degrees. He was sick rather than a killer, although I suspected Traudl had been pressing his buttons. By morning a cool sponge-down, aspirin and nature had done their job and he was pretty well back to normal, puzzled and horrified at his own behaviour. Fragile peace descended once again on our small community.

As soon as he was on his feet again, Chuck helped me move my American Quicksilver microlight, which had arrived with our furniture, to La Esperanza. Jack had a large waterproof barn and had been kind enough to offer to store the little plane. I'd been hoping to find a property with land suitable for a small landing strip, but Finca Tara wasn't ideal in this respect, as the only bit of orchard which could have been bulldozed level was a *very* 'short field', covered with trees, and with power lines at one end. The agricultural laws covering trees are quite tough and permission must be granted to fell them in rural areas; with this complication and so much else going on, a landing strip was right at the bottom of the list of priorities. I had to content myself with going up to the barn occasionally to stroke my flying lawnmower (the reliable Bombardier engine having been developed for more down-to-earth purposes than buzzing around the sky like an overweight bluebottle annoying the earth-bound).

James, although not a pilot himself, had the right qualifications (as an aeronautical engineer with many years in the Fleet Air Arm) to help me assemble and test it. Jack thought flying what amounted to a deckchair strapped to a lawnmower suspended from a scrap of canvas complete madness, but he did have one sensible suggestion: to try to find another pilot who would share expenses and flying time.

Jack was aware of our dire financial position and that the lack of firm bookings for our farmhouse holidays was taking its toll on optimism and enthusiasm, and he had another suggestion: maybe James and I would like to take over some of the maintenance and odd jobs at La Esperanza? His full-time estate worker, Paco, had given notice as he had reached the top of the waiting list to become a quarry-lorry driver, the height of ambition for local men, as they earned big money wrestling the lethally dangerous behemoths at piece-work speed to and from the vast building site known as the Costa del Sol. With Paco's departure there would be only one part-time worker and a gardener to look after the income-producing fruit trees, the large garden and the hundred and one problems caused by Jack's passion for gadgets.

This offer looked like manna from heaven. Paco had confided to James that Jack was a demanding employer, but we also knew him to be a kind and generous person. For a couple of days we had lived on the mandarins that he had heaped on us from the La Esperanza garden, a welcome gift as the cupboard was bare again. We thanked our stars for the opportunity to earn some cash; it had been a near run thing whether we, or the cats, ate that week.

Monday morning came, my first day of employment at La Esperanza, and I'd been asked to paint the newly-constructed dog pool. Jack and Maud had brought their two black Labradors from England and, as the dogs suffered from the heat at the height of summer, the decision had been made to build a large pool especially designed for them. The main pool was out of bounds because the chemicals irritated their skin and their hair clogged the filters.

I drove up through the village to La Esperanza through a foaming sea of delicate pink and pearly white almond and plum blossom. The sun shone and it felt pleasantly warm as I rolled up to Jack's video-controlled security gates, full of enthusiasm to start work. An array of eight unmarked buttons lay under the camera so I pressed the first row. Then the second row. Nothing happened, so I pressed them all in a different order and spoke into the voice grill. Still nothing. The drive vanished into the distance and the house was a quarter of a mile away hidden behind a bank of trees, but I tried a shout anyway, which was answered by distant barking – the dogs had heard my shouts but Jack hadn't. I looked for another way to get in, but the gate was high and spiked, so after another five minutes of fruitless button stabbing and shouting I went back to the village and phoned from Juan's Bar.

'Ah, there you are at last my dear,' boomed Jack. 'You're a bit late you know, it's ten past... I like people to be punctual.'

'I can't get in Jack, the gate phone isn't working.'

'Come on up Alex, you must have pressed the wrong button. I'll let you in.'

Back to the security-fenced estate and the imposing entrance with its curved walls swathed with carmine bougainvillaea and pierced by window-like openings guarded by *rejas*, the ornamental anti-burglar bars of southern Spain. This time the camera lit up when I pressed the buttons and the electric gates started opening jerkily. The car was halfway through when one of the gates abruptly reversed and started closing again, giving the rear bumper a ringing whack. Rattled, I drove down the sparkling-white gravel drive edged with palms and drew up outside the large two-story house with its 'Southern Belle' double staircase. Stepping out of the car, I was roughly jostled by the two Labradors in a barking whirl, studded with impressively gleaming fangs. They weren't the friendly bumbly Labradors I was used to, although they backed away obediently enough when Jack called them.

'That's right Alex, let them get to know you,' he exclaimed approvingly as my proffered hands were sniffed and then engulfed by enthusiastic tongues. Sabre released my hand with just a lick, but William's teeth closed retriever-soft on my fingers in a subtle warning as he grinned up at me, brown eyes limpidly innocent.

'Have to keep them shut up when we've got visitors,' Jack remarked with a fond smile. 'They can be little beggars if they don't know you.'

'After what happened to the postman...' Maud muttered.

Jack's eyebrows drew together in a frown. 'It wasn't the boys' fault Maudie, the Spaniards don't know how to treat 'em. It's no good running, that's just asking for trouble. If he'd only stood his ground...'

'And that poor man from the village...' Maud continued, pursing her lips.

Jack's face darkened. 'That drunken dago lout. If he ever turns up here again...'

Maud giggled under her breath as she turned to me. 'A lad from the village somehow climbed over the fence in the night and went to sleep in the Range Rover there,' she waved a hand at the vehicle, 'but the dogs wouldn't let him get out again – he was pretty desperate by the time we got up late on Sunday morning and heard him shouting.'

'Bloody man, smoking in my car, couldn't get rid of the smell for weeks,' grumbled Jack.

Maud nearly disappeared under the canine tsunami as we went into the house.

'Come in dear and have a cup of coffee.' She leant towards me confidingly, her kind face puzzled. 'You know, it's so nice to have someone to talk to. People don't call very often.'

I was beginning to see why.

❧

Jack filled the dog pool with water just as the weather became rather chilly again, but we all congregated to watch the dogs enjoy their first dip in their £8,000 purpose-built spa. The result was disappointing: they jumped up on the broad ledge circling the round pool, ran around and around barking, and even ventured to stand on the ramp that dipped under the surface, but nothing would persuade them to get *into* the water. Jack invited them to get in, then ordered them to get in, then threw sticks and ordered them to get in, then shouted at them to 'Bloody get in, or else...'

But they gazed alternately at their master's face and the sparkling blue water, wagged their tails and flatly refused to put so much as a paw in the purified-to-drinking-quality, chemical-free ionised water. To be fair, from their point of view it was definitely a swimming pool, and they weren't allowed in swimming pools; also, being gun dogs, they were accustomed to dark dirty water with nice muddy banks. It seemed like an expensive impasse, but Jack had owned a large dairy business and was used to executive decisions and personnel management techniques.

'Alex, get in the pool and help the boys,' he boomed. 'We aren't getting anywhere like this. William has always been a bit water-shy.'

'Me?...but, Jack...' I whined, 'I haven't got my swim-suit... the water's freezing...I'm, umm, just getting over a cold.' All of these statements were true, but what I was actually thinking was that either or both of the dogs were more than capable of delivering a nasty nip if forced into something they most certainly didn't want to do.

'Wouldn't they come to you if you were in the water?' I asked innocently.

'Uh, well, Maudie and I don't swim you see Alex, so just be a good girl and let's get on with it.'

His face was darkening with disapproval at my timidity. 'Oh well,' I thought, 'if I want any more work here I suppose I'd better just do it. At least my tetanus shots are up-to-date.' Reluctantly I trudged down the ramp into the frigid water, and as Jack gave him a mighty heave from the ledge, I yanked Sabre's legs out from under him, and in the mêlée fell over backwards. The next minute I was under water with a large, powerful dog using me as a convenient stepping-stone while he considered his options. When I resurfaced Sabre was swimming strongly around the pool with every sign of enjoyment; I, on the other hand, being a poor swimmer with a strong dislike of putting my head underwater, was coughing and spouting water like a defective fountain.

'Well done Alex, now for William,' shouted Jack encouragingly.

'...*coff coff, eughhhaargh*...' I replied elegantly, bringing up another gush of water. 'Wait a min...'

Too late. William was sailing through the air towards me, his body twisting desperately away from the inevitable. He wasn't as big or heavy as Sabre, but he had a great deal more momentum. Together we sank to the bottom and I had another intimate, lingering look at the quality of the paintwork I'd so recently completed. William had much sharper nails than Sabre, a fact I was made painfully aware of when he scraped every single one of them down my body in blind panic as he attempted to get his head out of the water. We clawed our way to the surface as one and dog-paddled with grim determination towards the ramp, despite Jack's cries of disappointment at our lack of form.

William didn't seem to bear any grudge towards me. In fact, our shared dislike of having our heads underwater made us friends, and over the next few days I spent half an hour each day in the dogs' pool supporting him in the water, as the poor dog simply lacked confidence in his own swimming ability. Like initially reluctant kids, the dogs soon started enjoying themselves and by the end of the week it was impossible to get them out of the water – they played like seals until dark.

The dog pool wasn't the end of Jack's piscinal worries: to keep the grandchildren happy, he had installed solar heating for the main pool, but despite an Olympic-size bank of panels the water was a mere four degrees warmer than ours, and our six foot deep pool was decidedly chilly. The technicians were called from Malaga and blood ran in the gutters as Jack demanded action and warm water in equal quantities. Cowed by his fury and the knowledge that he had spent a great deal of money to heat the pool out of season, they installed another two panels at no extra cost and fine-tuned the massive installation as best they could, despite the heavy cloud cover that blanketed the Costa del Sol that day.

By this time I was renewing the exterior paintwork of La Esperanza, the contract awarded possibly as an apology for the dog pool double ducking. It was going rather slowly due to the many delightful distractions offered by La Esperanza and its owners; Maud called me down off the ladder for endless cups of coffee and meals, and Jack, who enjoyed sporting pursuits, regarded me as an extra gun, dog or beater, as the occasion demanded. On a typical morning a roar would be heard in the distance. 'Sabre! William! Alex! ... Alex, where the hell are you? Come here quick!'

Scuttling down the ladder, I'd find a tree-rat hunt in progress in the vine arbour, and another hour would be wasted as the dogs and I flushed the rats out of privet hedges and the vines while Jack picked them off with a rifle. But there was a far more serious pest than rats, as we were to find out.

Spring was just around the corner and Maud had requested some freshening of the interior paintwork as part of her spring-clean. As usual I had arrived at 9am, but Maud's normally cheery greeting was subdued and her face was glum.

'It's William, he's at the vet's...I'm ever so worried,' she said in reply to my enquiry. 'Go up and see Jack, he's in his study – here, take this tea and toast. See if you can persuade him to have his breakfast.'

Jack looked up from the book he was reading, face grim. 'Morning Alex, shut the door. Did Maudie tell you about poor William?'

'Just that he's with the vet. What's happened?'

'I haven't told Maudie yet, it would break her heart, but we may well lose him.' Jack rubbed his hand over his face, trying to hide a less than stiff upper lip. 'The vet's operating right now, we should know something by midday.'

'Poor old William – but he's strong as an ox Jack, what's the problem?'

'Gangrene of the tongue. He was missing all yesterday morning, then came in frothing at the mouth, shaking his head. Wouldn't eat, so I knew there was something wrong, but I couldn't see anything in his mouth. Phoned the vet and he said, 'Have you got any of those processionary caterpillars in your trees?' I expect you've seen those gauzy nests in the pine trees down by the fence? Rushed him down to the surgery straight away but his tongue was already affected.' Jack pointed at the book on his desk. 'Just reading up about the bloody things, didn't know they were as dangerous as hell.'

He handed me the book and I skimmed through the chapter:

Caterpillars feed at night and return to the nest at dawn...
...end of winter they leave the nest...
...following each other in head to tail processions...
... over the ground processions of over 300...
...looking for soft soil in which to pupate...
... sting with highly urticating hairs anyone who molests them...
...rashes, allergic response, eye irritation, blistering...
...touch a nest and the dust of the hairs sticks to face and skin causing...
...burning the nests causes corrosive vapour...goggles...mask
...dangerous to children and pets...
...should not be touched...

'Good god Jack, I thought they were just caterpillars, not the insect equivalent of napalm,' I exclaimed in horror.

'Well, we're going to sort them out my girl. There's Sabre to think of as well.' Jack went to the gun cabinet and unlocked it, bringing out two shotguns. 'Go and get goggles, masks and the flame-thrower from the shed Alex. We've got work to do.'

Armed, goggled, masked and hatted, we approached the pine trees and their deeply unpleasant inhabitants. Close to, the damage caused by the caterpillars was easy to see. Dead brown fronds drooped where they had been feeding and at the ends of the branches hung gauzy, voluminous, pear-shaped bags of dirty white silk and leaves, as big as a man's head. On the ground were a couple of skeins of caterpillars, velvety brown and covered with stiff whitish hairs, each caterpillar with its head touching the rear of the one in front in an unbroken conga line which twisted and turned around stones and over twigs.

'We'll deal with these on the ground later,' Jack said, indicating the flame-thrower, 'after we mop up the nests.'

Throwing the 12 bore up to his shoulder, he started firing at the nests in the treetops.

I don't like 12 bores much, finding them too heavy, noisy and painful if not positioned correctly in the shoulder, but this wasn't the moment to be girly and squeamish about a little excruciating pain.

Bursts of gunfire continued all morning as the nests tumbled down through the branches, the frass inside the nests puffing out and raining down on us until every bit of uncovered skin itched and burned. Finally there were no more nests to be seen in the tattered pines and the roaring *flammenwerfer* lit the darkness of the spinney as Jack made sure the fallen nests and their inmates were destroyed.

It was a huge relief when Maud walked down from the house to tell us the vet had phoned and he was pretty sure William was going to be all right.

When I drove back home, the village seemed strangely quiet and deserted, with doors closed and blinds drawn. It was eerily like the scene from a Western where the baddies ride into town: even the usual stray dogs lying in the road had vanished, and to my annoyance the little village store was closed, a most unusual event as the proprietors lived above the shop. Surely they couldn't think the gunfire, protracted though it was, had been some sort of gang warfare going on up at t' big house, could they?

The caterpillars had been dealt with in the nick of time, as there was a sudden hot spell, just the sort of weather that would have brought them out in their hundreds to weave their way through the woods in search of a suitable site to pupate. But the sun brought another problem.

It had been a cold night, but like the preceding day the sun felt incredibly hot on my shoulders as I got the ladders out of the shed. Walking to the house, I was puzzled to see the swimming pool was capped with a roiling white mist, and if an apparition of the Lady of the Lake waving Excalibur had stepped out of the vapour it wouldn't have looked out of place. But instead it was the fist-waving figure of my employer that surged out of the billowing cloud like a temperamental elderly rock star having technical problems with the dry-ice blower.

'Put your hand in the water Alex, feel the temperature. The bloody water's boiling!' Jack was dancing with rage as he kicked the loungers aside, towing shreds of steam behind him like a granny's shawl. 'I asked those stupid sods for *warmer* water, not a sodding Turkish bath! Half the solar panels have cracked. It's a total cock-up. I'll have someone's b******s for this!'

It was true, the water was hot: therapeutic, muscle relaxing, almost Japanese tub hot. If only we'd had a handy football team, Jack could have done them proud in the early bath department.

❧

James and I always wore our oldest clothes when we were working at La Esperanza and didn't worry too much about our appearances, so when Maud mentioned that she was having a smart lunch party for a few well-heeled locals in aid of a local charity, we saw no reason to dress differently from normal. We knew they would be in the barbecue area and that we would be on the other side of the estate. James was in his boiler-suit and looking a little less than suave with a two-day growth of beard as he worked on the many water pumps that supplied the irrigation to the mandarin trees. My paint-encrusted overalls and scraped-back-into-a-scrunchie hair went well with a cosmetic-free face and hands like brillo pads as I rubbed down the balustrades on the garden steps.

The constant beeping of the main gate video and the sound of tyres on gravel informed us that the guests were arriving, followed by a vivacious buzz indicating that they were having a good time.

'Alex, I've been telling everybody about you and James and your plans. You must come and meet them and have some lunch!' Jack stood on the terrace above me, beaming a wide and well-oiled host's smile.

'Uh, perhaps another time Jack. We really aren't dressed for this sort of do, thanks all the same.'

'No, no Alex, don't be silly and stand-offish. Nobody is worried about what you're wearing, they just want to meet you both...and there are a few people you've met already. Diego for one, and Janet.'

Jack was smiling, but he seemed quite determined. 'Come along now and bring James with you. He's down at the junction box, gate's been playing up again, only opening half-way. Nearly caught Bert and Dawn.'

Reluctantly, smoothing our hair and trying to knock some of the dust off our clothes, we walked down under the vine arbour and into the stone paved barbecue area, ringed with statuary and surrounded by shady arbutus, jacaranda trees and flower beds. Linen cloths covered the stone tables, laid with crystal glasses and vases of flowers, while a sumptuous buffet lunch was laid out in the summer kitchen. The guests were equally sumptuous, one or two even running to hats, but the expressions on their faces were of friendly interest rather than disdain. Taking the proffered glasses of champagne, we moved forward to meet the people who would become our friends, our allies, our advisers: the expats from around the world who lived and had businesses on the Costa del Sol.faces were of friendly interest rather than disdain. Taking the proffered glasses of champagne, we moved forward to meet the people who would become our friends, our allies, our advisers: the expats from around the world who lived and had businesses on the Costa del Sol.

6.
Friends & Neighbours

The solar panel technicians had made another visit, but despite all their efforts they couldn't reduce the water temperature much, so wisps of steam still drifted above the surface giving the appearance of a coolant pond at a nuclear power plant. Several of the guests at the charity do had brought their swimsuits for a dip after lunch – one of the ladies was heard to remark maliciously that she had already had a bath that morning thank you very much – but otherwise the warmth of the water was much admired by those people who hadn't started swimming for the season, because their own pool, like ours, was closer in temperature to the Serpentine than the Mediterranean.

Penny and Nigel, two of the swimmers, claimed Jack had spent thousands for nothing, as their pool was adequately heated by a great serpent of black garden hose laid out on a sunny terrace. Another couple chipped in to say their system – a south-facing, six-foot-high glass wall of discarded wine bottles with pipes running through it – also worked reasonably well. It was certainly a satisfactorily ecological end product of their drinking problem.

Penny and Nigel had started a holiday business similar to ours on the other side of the village about a year previously, so they were a lot further along the road to success, but still finding things tough. Like us they had many problems with managing their bookings due to the lack of a telephone. They had, to a degree, got around it by dealing with a recognised company in the field who managed the letting details of the two self-catering villas they had built in the garden. Their biggest problem was the track down to their property from the main road, a rocky, rutted horror which wound around boulders and over a tiny bridge before scrambling up a steep scree slope to the parking area. It didn't need much rain to make the track impassable and the removal truck carrying their furniture had had to park on the main road while all their goods and chattels were ferried through a downpour by a farmer with a tractor and trailer.

Luckily, most visitors came in summer when dust was the main hazard.

Both Penny and Nigel were ex-Army: he was an engineer and she had been a military policewoman, and they were self-sufficient and hard working. To make a garden, they had cleared rocks from the land for months, piling them up into attractive retaining walls for the terraced flower and vegetable beds. Penny was usually to be found with her bottom in the air in the garden, planting hedges and beds to a design carefully worked out on squared paper.

They were generous with their help and advice, and we soon became friends. Penny had learnt Spanish at the University of Seville, so not only spoke it fluently, but also understood Spanish customs and peculiarities. She warned us that our workers had done a sufficiently major job to expect a *bandera* (a party, usually a sit-down meal involving *paella* and plenty of wine) before they left Finca Tara for the last time.

So it was arranged. Chuck and Traudl were also invited to the celebration as Chuck had done quite a lot of work and Traudl, whose Spanish was fluent, had been invaluable at translating documents and helping out when technical communications really broke down. Having borrowed a large *paellera* – a flat two-handled pan – I spent the morning making the traditional *paella* with pork, chicken, shellfish and saffron rice, dotted with peas and shreds of red pepper. I was nervous about cooking a Spanish speciality for such an experienced and critical audience, much more nervous than if I'd been cooking for a smart dinner party. But at least the dining hall looked nice and I'd laid the table with a linen cloth and the best glasses. At 2pm the men trooped in, almost unrecognisable with their immaculately clean shirts and combed hair, hands washed and nails manicured with their pocket-knives. I was touched when José handed me a bunch of beautifully fragrant flowers and almost felt sorry that the gang would be breaking up – but we couldn't afford them any longer, although there was still a lot to do.

The lunch went well, although Traudl rather spoilt the atmosphere by complaining about the unhygienic habits of Spanish men. Looking around at Antonio Manuel, Paco and José, with their shining faces and Sunday-best shirts brought specially to wear for lunch, I couldn't agree with her and was thankful that they didn't understand English. To add insult to injury, she had her little dog on her lap and was feeding it from her plate, which I found slightly revolting. This was illogical as I did the same with the cats, but at least I only did it in private!

We got through a few bottles of wine, followed by coffee and liqueurs. Everybody was in a good mood when the *bandera* wound up and the men were paid their last wage. To my stunned amazement and admiration they then changed back into work clothes and put in another couple of hours work, teetering on narrow planks above the courtyard as they fitted guttering. James had arranged to keep Paco on to help him with re-roofing, a two-man job that unfortunately couldn't be postponed any longer as the roof leaked like a sieve every time we had heavy rain.

First the pretty but porous old terracotta tiles were carefully removed and stacked for re-use, then the soaking sand mixture on which they had been bedded was shovelled away until the concrete roof was bare. It was then easy to see how the water was getting in, as there were several cracks running the length of the roof. These were made good and an impermeable membrane was fitted, consisting of thick tarry strips welded together with a blow-torch until they were tailored to the roof in one piece like a giant rubber pixie-hood. Completed, it must have weighed over half a ton and sat there happily enough. It was two days of hard heavy work and James was exhausted as he came in to supper on the second evening.

'Glad I've got the membrane finished,' he said, flopping down grey-faced with fatigue. 'Just in time by the look of it. There are some big clouds coming in.'

'The rain won't affect it then, it won't get blown about?'

'No, nothing will affect it, it's tough and hellish heavy. You helped me get the rolls up on the roof, they weren't light were they?'

I was a tiny bit concerned about the wind, as a freak gust had wrapped the terrace awning around the chimney stack out of a clear blue sky, but we had no idea how powerful the rotors rolling down the mountain behind us could be until a few hours later when we awoke to a monstrous, grinding tearing noise. We rushed outside thinking 'earthquake', to find the night quiet and still, but the membrane lay crumpled and useless in the courtyard like a dead elephant.

The garden looked like a set for a crummy Greek movie, with an avenue of broken and toppled columns dragging down the vine arbour. The brick-built vine arbour was reasonably cheap and easy to replace, but none of the membrane could be salvaged. This was a major blow in the cash department and, reluctantly, we had to let Paco go.

We would have to work for Jack for another month to get the money together for more materials, but James finally finished the roof just in time for our first paying guests.

∾

The Trubshaws had decided to hire a car from the airport, so we knew what time they would arrive. The day flew past as we swept and polished, checked and double-checked. It was a big moment and we wanted everything to go smoothly so we could welcome our first guests in a professional and polished manner.

With a quarter of an hour to go, I threw open the two halves of the big wooden front door into the central courtyard. There was a hissy scuffling behind me; looking around, I saw Luigi playing horrible cat games with a small viper in the dining hall, throwing it up in the air, then pouncing as it landed and tried to escape.

I screamed and flapped my hands at him. Luigi gave me a look of utter disgust and dropped the viper, walking away with an insolent glance backwards as the snake grabbed its opportunity and slithered into the nearest hole, which happened to be the middle of the draught-proofing rubber channel that was nailed to the bottom of the front door. Nothing would shift it. The snake ignored knuckles rapping on the door, twigs gingerly shoved up the channel, pleas, curses, prayers... Only the faintest of hisses and a glittering eye gave the game away as James and I panicked. What if it slithered out of the door as our guests arrived? What if it fanged them? What if it crawled into their room off the courtyard and into their shoes or luggage? And how would we put it to them?

'Excuse my mentioning it Mr and Mrs Trubshaw, but there's a slightly irritable viper wandering around the house, but don't worry, it's unlikely that the bite will harm you unless you have a heart condition. Uh oh, I'm very sorry to hear that, Mr Trubshaw...only six weeks ago you say, and you came here for a nice quiet holiday to recuperate?'

No, it just wouldn't do. It seemed all too likely that they would leave, at best, or sue us if the worst happened. Then I had a flash of inspiration and ran for my shotgun. With shaking hands we loaded it and James poked it up the channel hoping the rubber would absorb any ricochet. With a muttered apology to the unfortunate reptile, he pulled the trigger.

If the Trubshaws wondered why our front door appeared to have been gnawed by giant rats, why a strange ichor dripped from the draught-proofing, or why we lobbed rocks at a poor little black and white cat that lurked in the bushes, they were too polite to mention it. Their holiday passed without incident, they appeared to enjoy it, and even recommended us to their friends.

Luigi seemed determined to wipe out the local wildlife single pawed. His next mistake was to fall into the swimming pool and I was sympathetic enough until I spotted a young bat in the water, on the point of drowning. Fortunately it was just wet and not injured, and it flew off as soon as it was fished out and thrown into the air – but I put two and two together and it equalled Luigi taking a flying leap at the bats that swooped out of the algarroba tree beside the pool every evening to hunt mozzies.

The algarroba is an interesting tree; hung with long brown bean-like pods filled with a sweet red mush containing ten identical seeds. It's said to have been used for human and animal feed from prehistoric times and it's still used as an alternative to chocolate. The seeds are so uniform that the Moors used them in the balance to weigh precious stones; they were the original 'carat' weight. Ulla had said that at harvest time the gypsies would come and offer to pick the crop – the pods turned out to be our easiest cash crop.

A few more bookings were coming in now and as we got into the swing of it, looking after our guests became easier. So when three rather wealthy and high-powered middle-aged ladies arrived in October for their annual get-together, we welcomed them with confidence. October is generally a pleasant month in Andalucia; warm enough to sit on the terrace and sunbathe, have a leisurely lunch in the garden, enjoy a glass of *cava* and some olives by the pool, and sometimes even warm enough at midday to have a little dip. The three ladies did all these things and had long rambles through the *campo* taking photographs and chatting.

As James and I fell into bed on their last night after a good dinner, we congratulated ourselves that everything had gone so well. Some particularly malicious god with a warped sense of humour must have overheard.

The day had been a bit humid and overcast, and as we went to bed the clouds were piling up in menacing ramparts to the west. As we sleepily chatted about our day, the first rumble of thunder rolled around the basin formed by the surrounding hills, punctuated by a flash of lightning. Rain pattered on the roof, but since the roof was now waterproof it didn't cause the butterfly-tummy of dread we had suffered before whenever there was a rainstorm. The storm moved closer until the thunder and lightning flashes were almost simultaneous. It was right overhead now and the rain was sheeting down so hard the pattering had turned to drumming and the wind howled in the gaps left by the thunder.

There was a crack so loud and so close that our eardrums reverberated, followed by a rat-tat-tatting so violent it was like being in a steel dustbin being hosed down by an Uzi. We abandoned any pretence of getting to sleep and I huddled under the bedclothes, beginning to feel very frightened indeed.

We were sleeping in the 'old garage', which was at the end of the terrace but separate from the house, and James felt he should check whether the ladies were all right.

'Damn, the electricity is out,' James muttered, trying the bedside lamp. 'They've got candles in their rooms, but they might appreciate a cup of tea or something. Nobody could sleep in this.' Illuminated by the sheet lightning he hopped around pulling on his jeans.

'See if the cats are okay, they may be nervous with the thunder,' I replied, glad to leave it to James.

He wrestled open the door and I heard an exclamation as he stepped out onto the terrace. There was a brief pause and then a piercing yell cut through the howl and boom of the storm. I leaped out of bed and wrenching open the door looked out. The terrace was white, inches deep in hailstones as big as grapes, and my husband was lying in a bed of bougainvillea and cactus groaning pitifully.

'Look out... it's sheet ice, slippery as hell. I went head-first into this bed of cactus, hurts like buggery,' he moaned as I tried to help him out.

'Oh lord, come on, we've got to get in the house. At least there are some lamps and candles there.' Already I was soaked to the skin, and my dressing gown wasn't much protection against the freezing rain.

The courtyard was knee-deep in hailstones and water, which was seeping through the bullet-riddled front door in a brown trickle, oozing through chinks in the window frames, puddling on the tiles and meandering through the house leaving a layer of brown, muddy goo. As we piled the rugs on the furniture we found Luigi cowering under the sofa, but of Smoo there was no sign.

'That idiotic old cat, he'll catch his death out there. I'll have to go and see if I can find him,' I muttered, peering out into the water-loud darkness with a torch that seemed about as useful as a cat-flap on a submarine. After what seemed like hours, but was probably only five minutes, of calling and looking in his favourite hiding places, I found him crouched in the brick dog kennel Ulla had built by the gate, looking tiny and gaunt and a bit desperate as the water rose around his legs. Taking him firmly under my arm, he was rushed indoors to be rubbed down in a towel, a liberty he repaid by scratching bloody weals across my hand.

The three ladies were huddled together in one double bed, all as terrified as I was but being brave and cheerful about it in a very British way.

Next morning we were all a bit subdued and red-eyed as we had a rather hurried breakfast and went outside to see what damage had been done. The little *río* at the bottom of our land was now a raging river, and the valley echoed to the dull thunder of water that sounded like an approaching train, carrying trees, bamboo groves, old refrigerators and rubbish down to Malaga and the sea. Antonio's *huerta* was totally underwater and his well house was gone. We were a bit luckier, as our well house and the expensive electric pump it housed were miraculously still there.

A 30-foot piece of the Railway Road itself had collapsed into the river where it passed over a culvert and the hundreds of tons of tarmac and road had vanished without trace. All that was left was the pitiful detritus of any major flood: a tiny pink plastic shoe, a refrigerator, tyres and a dead dog in a white Seat. It was an awe inspiring sight – shocked people were gathered in small groups exchanging news of damage and missing people and property. La Cabra was later declared the epicentre of a storm that had killed eleven people.

In the village we heard more bad news; the little stream that flowed through La Esperanza and through the village was now a thundering torrent that had confined Jack and Maude to their house, and drowned a flock of 80 goats in a shed behind La Porrita, a new bar and restaurant that had just been built as a rival attraction to Juan's Bar.

The only good news was that the airport would open at midday and that our ladies would be able to catch their flight back to the West Country. We had to laugh when we read their entry in our visitor's book: *'Thank you – this has been the most exciting holiday we've ever had.'*

7.
Cosmic, Man!

Christmas was approaching again and we were looking forward to a proper celebration: we had a full house booked in for the holiday consisting of a family with two small children and Hortense, this time without her Viscount. We broke out the Scandinavian tree decorations to hang on the olive 'tree', a big sucker pulled from the trunk of the oldest olive tree on the land. We liked the peace connotations of the olive, especially at Christmas, a time that seems to provoke the worst sort of family warfare.

The dead trees felled and logged by Keef and Becky during their stay were now used to keep a big fire going all day in the living room, and to feed the wood-burner James had installed in the dining hall. Despite the protestations of many visitors to Spain that 'you don't need heating on the Costa del Sol', we found that you most certainly do need it in a mountain *finca* with no damp course and leaky windows and doors.

Most homes had portable gas fires running on a *bombona*, but I found they made rooms stuffy and caused headaches, as well as adding a pint of water to the atmosphere every hour – not exactly what you need in a damp house, so we went for The Three Tree Warms instead. The first warm was when you cut the tree down, the second when you cut it up and the third when you burnt it.

Christmas Day dawned bright and sunny and was so hot by midday that I decided to have a swim; this was a huge mistake as the water temperature bore no resemblance to the air temperature, and I went down with bronchitis two days later. The Christmas lunch was cooked with numb blue fingers and afterwards everybody went for a walk. The mandarins and oranges were ripe, so the family party went down to the *río* where the best trees grew and picked a sack full of fruit for the house.

Dominic, their four-year-old redheaded whirlwind rushed back into the house with an orange balanced on his palm and his face alight. 'Look Alex, look, a *real* orange wot I picked!'

For a brief second I saw through a child's eyes again the colour, the texture, the spurt of tongue tingling juice, the miracle.

As we didn't spray our trees against pests, it was necessary to examine the fruit rather carefully for inhabitants – a little brown puncture mark meant there would be a maggot inside – but we didn't spoil Dominic's miracle by pointing out these drawbacks to *real* fruit.

There were plenty of parties over Christmas and our friends were generous about asking houseguests, even including our paying guests, which they very much appreciated. You know they've had a good time when they book for the following year!

At Jack and Maud's Christmas party we got to know Freddie and Felicity rather better, having met them at the charity lunch earlier in the year. Freddie had the unkind but apt nickname of Fat Freddie – he was a large and athletic man who had become enormous with the passing years. He was also highly intelligent, a great raconteur and a skilled amateur artist. Felicity was a lovely lady; blonde, bubbly and always cheerful, but her natural optimism was being tested by Freddie's back problems, which were deteriorating despite treatment. He had invested in various cushions and remedies, a new mattress and a corset, but nothing seemed to work and he was spending an increasing amount of time in bed.

Penny and Nigel were showing off their latest acquisition, a radiophone. They'd scrimped and saved to buy it with some help from their parents, as everyone had agreed that it was essential for their business. It was a wonderful idea and was even portable, despite being the size of a breeze-block and about as heavy. We were frankly envious, but the £4,500 it cost was way beyond our budget – which, of course, they knew – and they generously offered to handle our messages. This was better than nothing, as we had been told by Telefonica (if you think BT is bad, try the Spanish version!) that we couldn't get a line for at least another three years. It says something about the deadly inertia of government monopolies that a community within sight of Malaga, needing a couple of hundred lines, must wait for three to four years before they would even consider upgrading the exchange.

Eager to sort out our English agent, we drove down to Penny and Nigel's straight after Christmas. The winter rains hadn't done anything for their track, which was a rock-strewn slalom on the way down and a skiddy crawl up again. Two-thirds of the way back to the main road James changed gear with a grating noise.

'Sorry, the clutch seems a bit manky,' he remarked. The next change just didn't happen at all. 'Uh oh, we've got a problem,' he announced, peering into the engine bay. 'The bloody engine's fallen out.'

The Fiat 128 we had bought to replace the Tonka truck was quite a nice little car, but not really up to the sort of tracks we had to use. It was a relief when Jack and Maude appeared in their Range Rover on their way to visit Nigel and Penny. For the second time we were towed home, but at least Jack knew where we lived. James beefed up the engine mountings but we always rather dreaded the Paris-Dakar Rally needed to collect our messages, in case the Fiat disembowelled itself again.

My pa, who was a keen gardener, had sent us some alpine strawberry seeds which had finally germinated and were growing in trays. When I took the covers off the trays some cat discovered them and performed a terrible act of vandalism, scratching over the evidence. I couldn't find either of our little darlings to get the forensic evidence from under their nails, but I suspected Smoo, who was quite partial to a dirt tray after his journey from England; there would have been a felicide had I found the evidence.

As a gardener I hated cats, and my thoughts dealt lovingly on blunderbusses loaded with nine inch nails and meticulously-crafted nooses woven from wolf spider silk. The delicate gardener/animal-lover interface was not improved by Scruffy – Freddie and Felicity's small hairy rescue dog – who was staying with us while Freddie was in hospital for tests on his back. Felicity kept him immaculate – washed and brushed and groomed – but maybe his early life had been in the *campo* because he loved mud and water and muck. When he stayed with us he would dig for hours in the garden and come back from walks with his long hair in mud dreadlocks, covered with burrs, goat droppings and ticks. Deliriously happy, his pleasure then was to lie on any bed, sofa or chair available, or even better, on all three of them.

Looking after Scruffy was nevertheless something we were happy to do as Freddie had taken a definite turn for the worse. He and Felicity were living in an apartment on the sea-front in Fuengirola and one day we called in shortly after Freddie's doctor had attended to give him a pain-killing injection. The doctor wanted Freddie to go into hospital for further tests to find the cause of his back pain and, as he was unable to walk, had called for an ambulance. The ambulance crew, two particularly weedy specimens, arrived with a stretcher but quickly discovered they couldn't even lift the patient, let alone get him out of the apartment. They had of course come up in the tiny lift to the fourth floor with the stretcher upright – there was no way it would fit in horizontally – but somehow the idea of stacking Freddy upright in the stretcher like a monstrous papoose didn't seem possible. We suggested carrying him down in a chair, but Freddie was too heavy even for a couple of weight-lifters, so the fire brigade was called in to advise. The apartment filled with large, efficient men kitted out in day-glo suits, helmets and breathing equipment, but even they were a bit puzzled as to how to remove Freddie. Finally they made a call to the mountain rescue team and shortly another group of large, efficient men in day-glo suits and rather smaller helmets arrived. By now we were spilling out into the communal hallway as Freddie laughed and joked with his 'removal men'.

A joint decision was made by the rescue services to get him out by means of a breeches buoy; the stretcher would be swung down to street level via a tackle set up on the roof of the building controlled by ropes. The mountain rescue team set to with a will. It was the first time they had attempted this manoeuvre in an apartment building, so it took quite a bit of discussion and consultation, but within a couple of hours they had the apparatus fixed on the roof and the balcony rail removed from the apartment below as it would have interfered with the cables. By now the police had cordoned off the road below and a large crowd was gathering as Felicity and I kept Freddie, the paramedics, firemen, police and mountain rescue team supplied with drinks and snacks.

Finally Freddie, looking a bit pale, was strapped firmly into a special stretcher with closed ends so he couldn't slide out, and was swung out into space, then carefully lowered. It went smoothly enough until Freddie got to the first floor where his bottom snagged on a large shop sign – even mountain rescue hadn't quite believed how heavy he was. There was a pause while the firemen rolled out a ladder and climbed up to unhook him, but at last, four hours after the doctor's call for an ambulance, waving to his audience like a film star, the patient was driven away to hospital

Various tests and a biopsy brought the worst sort of news: Freddie had cancer.

❧

A message via the radio phone brought some news to cheer us up: Michael and Gail were coming for a visit. James, Michael and I had worked for the same company and all four of us shared an enthusiasm for the sort of motorbikes that leave lots of oil on the floor, although I have to say the other three had lots of technical expertise while I just fell off into nettle-filled ditches occasionally. Michael had a laid-back attitude to life and an elfish sense of humour, and was notorious for the number of times he had been busted for having small quantities of wacky baccy. The force turned up at regular intervals to take tea with Michael, without any rancour on either side, and on these occasions he took a certain pleasure in offering them delicious hash cookies made by Gail that went down a treat. The forbidden weed was grown at the end of a long thin garden, guarded by a row of beehives, so all was well until the force engaged someone who had bees of his own – after that Michael concentrated more on the pleasures of alcohol.

Just before our friends' arrival, the gas boiler broke down so there was no hot water, but the £30 for a replacement heat exchanger was more than we could afford that week, so we decided to do without and boil kettles.

Their first day coincided with a spell of perfect spring weather and as they both enjoyed hiking we decided to drive to Torre Alqueria and walk up the river-bed track that I'd first taken with Diego and Paddy to view the mountain-top cottage. It was as lovely as I remembered, with the sandy river bed fringed with pink oleander and the hills on either side carpeted with swathes of glorious wild flowers. We walked up to the cottage I'd liked so much and to the threshing floor above it, which was a great circle cut into the hillside paved with rounded cobbles. Enjoying the bee-buzzing, thyme-scented breeze on our faces, it was easy to imagine what it would have looked like a hundred years ago, with donkeys circling the threshing floor pulling the wooden sleighs, their under surface studded with sharp flints that bruised the ears of corn and released the grain. You can still buy these sleighs in Fuengirola flea market or antique shops, made into coffee tables or restaurant ornaments.

In the distance we heard the tinkle of goat bells. Shepherds spend a lot of money on these bells, each one a different tone, so that the goats make surreal music as they move. Borne on the wind it's an enchanted Fairyland sound, once heard never forgotten.

We were all pretty well away with the fairies as we went down the hill again, a mixture of crystal-pure air, stunning views, flowers and sunshine had put us all in a mood for magic, so when I spotted something glinting in the river bed I almost knew what it was before picking it up.

'James, come and look at this,' I exclaimed, 'it looks just like the heat exchanger off our boiler.'

'You're right, it does...and it doesn't look as though it's damaged either... I can't think for a minute it would work...but it's worth a try.'

'Cosmic, man!' exclaimed Michael.

Clutching the heat exchanger, we walked on past a flock of goats. With a shout, a figure leapt out of the bushes beside the track and warmly embraced and kissed James, followed by the rest of us. I'm not sure that Michael and Gail appreciated being soundly kissed by a goat-fragrant satyr shepherd, but James explained that as José was practically family he had certain rights and privileges.

James fitted the *objet trouvé* heat exchanger, which after an initial bang, settled down and worked perfectly – it had indeed been a cosmic day.

ಷ

James was finding more work as word went around that he was a skilled and conscientious man who could put his hand to anything from welding to painting murals; but plumbing and electrical work was what most people wanted. He was asked to do the plumbing and wiring for a large extension on an old house in the village to help out the builder, an Austrian called Georg, and at last James found somebody he could work with.

Cielo Azul was a substantial looking house, but after thirty years the systems needed replacing and Joan wanted a new kitchen. James helped Georg pull out the old cabinets and to their horror they found an army of giant cockroaches lurking underneath. At first they killed the scuttling horrors with hammers, but that wasn't quick enough, so they broke into a frenzied *tarantella* in their work boots, a dance said to have originated from stamping on tarantulas. But it was equally effective on cockroaches, although they were interrupted by a puzzled Joan.

'What on earth are you doing?' she demanded, clutching their mugs of tea and biscuits, 'I can hear you from the other end of the house.' She looked down at the carpet of insects and screamed, and the tea shot into the air.

'Never mind the tea, Joan,' said Georg, 'we go to the bar. I need a drink, and anyway the porks are smelling.' The one drawback to Cielo Azul was the pig farm opposite.

Don and Janet, who were among the first foreigners in La Cabra, had a large and comfortable house equipped to Canadian tastes, with a huge fridge-freezer, a fancy coffee machine and a large TV to view taped ball games. Don was a writer, with a garage stuffed with thousands of reference books and novels. His telephone-bell repeater system, which had been installed by the Spanish gardener, had started ringing continuously during a rainstorm, then exploded and set fire to the papers on his desk. Don was nervous that it might also incinerate his precious books in the garage, so he asked James to rewire the system. Janet mentioned that she rather fancied a fountain in their interior courtyard, but couldn't find one that she liked. James and I sketched out some ideas, and soon Don and Janet had a beautiful mosaic fountain and the sound of tinkling water whenever they wished – which lead them to think about what else they wanted.

Don's mother had recently come to live with them and one of the suggestions was an extension to the house in the form of a tower. James and I met Lucille, an elegant and charming elderly lady who looked like a doll beside her well-built son. She was quite frail and hadn't recovered from her husband's death some six months previously, so when Don and Janet had to go to Gibraltar overnight on business, they asked Penny to look after Lucille.

I was working at La Esperanza when James turned up to say that Penny was having a problem with Lucille and needed a hand.

'What do you mean, a problem – has she fallen or something?' I asked.

'Well, no... not exactly,' James scratched his chin. 'I can't really believe it, but Penny claims that Lucille was sitting on the garden wall shouting about being kept prisoner...and she couldn't get the old girl down, so when Rick drove past she flagged him down and he managed to coax her off the wall, but then she did a runner up the road with Rick in pursuit...'

I laughed disbelievingly. 'Oh come on James, they must have been pulling your leg. Lucille is 82 years old, so how's she going to get onto a six foot wall?'

'Yeah, well, that's what I thought – but Penny has sure as hell got her knickers in a twist.'

I sighed and put the paintbrush down. 'Okay, god knows what we can do about it, but I suppose we'd better go and see what's going on.'

Penny was on the phone trying to find a doctor who would attend and didn't seem to be having much luck.

'Look, we'll see if we can find them and get Lucille back to the house,' said James. We went in the direction they had taken and shortly afterwards split up as the road branched. I walked on in the hot sunshine, peering into gardens and driveways until the village houses petered out into countryside. I was about to give up and go back when I spotted Rick sitting on a bale of hay in the middle of a field mopping his face with a hanky, with Lucille standing about 20 feet away examining a poppy.

'Thank god you're here,' Rick gasped, 'I'm just about at the end of my tether.' Sweat was running down his sun-reddened face. 'We've been running all over the countryside for four hours. It's awful, if anyone comes near she starts throwing stones at them, and she's had a bit of a go at me!' He waved an arm scored with nail marks. Rick looked exhausted and distressed; he wasn't a spring chicken himself.

'Ummm, that arm doesn't look too good... you've done your

bit Rick, go on back to Don's place, and if you see James let him know where we are.'

'But I can't leave you here alone with her...' Rick started.

'Oh yes you can,' I replied firmly. 'I'll be perfectly all right and it won't help anybody if you get sunstroke.'

Rick reluctantly turned to go and I cautiously approached Lucille. 'Hello Lucille, it's hot out here isn't it? Wouldn't you like to go home and get a cool drink?'

She looked up from the flower and smiled. 'Hello dear, I know you, don't I...it's Louella isn't it? You're married to the Parsons boy and live down at Sioux Falls?'

'Yeah...er, that's right Lucille,' I said, wondering if I should attempt a Louella-type accent, but rapidly abandoned the idea. 'Shall we go home now?'

'I don't think so dear. Frank won't be back from the office yet.'

My heart sank – Frank was her recently deceased husband. Lucille looked cool and composed, and although she wasn't wearing a hat her face wasn't even faintly pink.

'Frank likes salads in this weather,' she continued, 'especially beetroot with a mustard dressing and a few rollmops.'

For twenty minutes we chatted pleasantly about everything and nothing: cooking, how to make fresh lemonade, the best way to fold shirts.

'Perhaps we should go back now and start getting Frank's supper,' I said and, gently taking her arm, steered her towards the road. In the blink of an eye, everything changed.

'You leave Frank alone, I know what you're after,' Lucille snarled, pulling her arm away. 'I've heard about you and the goings on...' Her pleasant face had changed into an unrecognisable mask of hatred and her eyes glared with a red light. 'If you don't leave Frank alone I'm going to call the cops.' She headed at a fast pace up the road and branched off into a side road I didn't know. She didn't appear to hear anything I said, or if she did, it didn't have any relevance to the scene unfolding behind her eyes.

Then what I'd been dreading happened: we came to a little group of houses with children playing outside and Lucille bent down and picked up a stone.

'*Chicos*, go inside your house, now, please!' I said, and the kids obediently stopped playing and turned away with puzzled glances. One of the mothers frowned and came towards us and Lucille wound up and let fly, the stone just missing her. I made a twirling motion with my finger at my temple behind the old lady's back and the mother backed away. Again I tried to take Lucille's arm, but she broke into a little stumbling run and we were off again.

It was over an hour before the car with James and Penny found us, with the doctor and his assistant bringing up the rear. We gently herded Lucille into a corner of a field and she was quieting down nicely when the doctor held his hypodermic up and examined the tip. With a scream of rage Lucille broke through the cordon of our arms and was a 100 yards away before we caught up. It felt all wrong to subject her to this treatment, but it took four of us to hold one ancient, frail woman while the doctor injected her with a sedative.

8.
Mountain Krauts

Everyone went home or back to work, satisfied that Lucille was safe and that the hospital would keep her in until she was thoroughly checked out, mentally stabilised, re-hydrated and possibly treated for sunstroke. So when Penny rang an hour later to say that the hospital had discharged Lucille and she and Nigel were bringing her home, it was greeted with total disbelief. We could only think that the hospital doctors, seeing this white-haired, sweet-faced, little *belle dame* quiet and compliant under the liquid cosh, simply refused to believe the story, putting it down to some form of mass hysteria.

Penny put the sleepy, still-tranquilised Lucille to bed and sat at the dining room table with Nigel, collating the lessons for the Spanish language course she was offering to foreigners eager to improve their conversational skills.

'Help, help me, *help*, they're trying to murder me!' The chillingly familiar cry came from the main road outside the house.

As they leaped up and ran outside, Lucille was already disappearing into the distance in the direction of the village, nightie fluttering as she swooped from side to side of the road. Nigel took off like a long dog in pursuit of an arthritic bunny and, catching up with the runaway he put his arms firmly around her, and ignoring the kicks and curses, frog-marched her home. Penny rang around for help, but found everyone unusually busy with urgent business; maybe we were all thinking much the same thought: Penny was younger, stronger and getting paid to look after Lucille, and if an ex-military policewoman couldn't control her, what chance did the rest of us have?

The upshot was that the hospital did finally admit Lucille and, after treatment, she returned home in a reasonably normal frame of mind. None of the doctors cared to comment on how she was able to climb a six-foot wall and run around in the blazing heat for six hours without any physical repercussions. There were the usual 'the mind has remarkable powers' platitudes; in other words, they still thought it was *our* collective mind that could do with a few sessions on the couch.

Lady Macbeth, as she was now known, seemed to be the only person unaffected by the heat; by 9am it was hot and by midday it was 114F on the pool terrace. Even the nights brought little relief; the sensual scents of jasmine and *Dama de Noche* wafting into the bedroom were strong enough to make the senses reel, but any ensuing amorous activity meant changing sweat-sodden sheets and yet another dip in the tarantula-infested pool.

The La Esperanza pool was so hot it could probably poach a salmon in 15 minutes, and a human being in 30, and ours was tepid, barely cool enough to quench sunburned skin. I was having second thoughts about the dips that helped me through the tandoori nights, since the morning trawl with the net usually turned up at least two or three drowned tarantulas. The searing African winds brought them out of their burrows and every shady nook and cranny hid a palm-sized hairy monster. Turning over pots or bags of fertiliser in the garden shed would always reveal at least one spider rearing up on its back legs, venom fangs at the ready. Chuck was bitten and showed us his swollen arm with some pride.

Even the cats were feeling the heat and Smoo would regularly batter down the bedroom door at five in the morning to demand that we do something about it. Despite the heat they liked long walks with us in the evening, sometimes going for a mile or more, with side trips up olive trees. Smoo would invariably feel a call of nature, which would mean endless stops while he carefully chose a suitable spot, and piteous wails as we finally walked on exasperated.

Antonio was envious of our cats. 'Just like dogs, just like dogs,' he muttered, sucking his teeth as we passed.

Dogs, however, don't generally bring in ten-inch centipedes as playmates. I nearly stepped on it in bare feet as Luigi patted it into my bleary-eyed barely-awake path; screaming I ran for the broom and brushed it outside, where we found two more even larger examples; this time we both screamed as centipede bites are very unpleasant and as bad as scorpion stings. Normally centipedes aren't much of a hazard, as they are small, nocturnal and secretive, but locally we harboured a creature much closer to the tropical model: eight to ten inches of grey-green malice with large poison fangs waving suggestively in a two-fingered gesture over its head. The thug was probably muttering the arthropod equivalent of 'who're *you* lookin' at Wully?' as he head-butted a scorpion out of that most desirable of nests – a pair of our sweaty workshoes left outside the back door to air overnight.

∾

My father sent packets of his favourite seeds. The aubergines, courgettes and peppers did well, but the tomatoes, although plentiful, weren't as good quality as I'd hoped and seemed rather tasteless. The yellow variety remained tiny and turned a strange orange as though sunburnt, but eaten with sugar as fruit – which is how they were first served in Europe – they were tasty enough. Puzzling over what was wrong with them and why my pa was so much better at growing vegetables than me, I looked up to find Antonio standing next to me, a grin on his face.

'You need more fertiliser, your soil is *malo,* very poor,' he said. '*Venga,* try this.' He plunged his hand into his pocket and brought out a big, juicy, dark red fruit and a bit of rag, with which he wiped his nose. The musty warm smell of fresh-picked tomato wafted over me as he held it out like a lover offering his beloved a *pomme d'amour*. I gulped. Antonio had worn the same pair of filthy working trousers all the time I'd known him and would no doubt wear them until they disintegrated, probably in the not too distant future. The seamed hand with its black-rimmed nails brought the perfect example of excreta-fertilised produce under my nose.

'*Pruebe lo*, try it, it's delicious, piquant,' he commanded.

It *was* delicious – it would be difficult to find a tastier or fuller-flavoured tomato with better texture and form. But for some reason I didn't really enjoy it.

≈

We ate our first peaches from the new tree in the *huerta* with great ceremony and enjoyment, all four of them. Wasps, a bit more alert than us, ate the other seven. Something was also grazing on the grapes – probably wasps again, of which we had an abundance nesting under the terracotta roof tiles. Brown paper bags were put over particularly promising bunches in the hopes of keeping a few for ourselves, rather than feeding every pest within ten miles. The geckos got a good telling off, as we never saw one actually catching any of the bluebottles, flies, greenbottles and wasps that infested the house. Instead they sat staring endlessly, their throats wobbling, until the flying thing they were stalking got bored with waggling its bottom and flirting its wings and flew away.

≈

The whole village looked forward to the annual La Cabra *feria*. The travelling fair set up camp on a piece of waste ground and Juan's Bar, The Goat & Garlic (La Porrita's nickname after the flood, since when goat had featured heavily on the menu) and Cristóbal's Bar braced themselves for a 24-hour non-stop marathon of eating and drinking.

The *feria* wasn't only a secular jolly, it also had a religious significance. The villagers took the statue of Saint Ana out of the chapel and paraded it around the village boundaries to bring good luck in the coming year. The little chapel had been derelict for years as the local priest said that it wasn't smart enough for services, but the villagers had made a big effort to collect money and the restoration was due to be finished in time for the *feria*. Workmen had been gilding, painting, and restoring the pews for months, and we could see the delightful result through the iron lace doors, framed in flowers and lit by banks of flickering votive candles.

The priest had promised a dedicatory mass during the *feria*, so we were all a bit taken aback when he turned up in his civvies looking like someone's gardener and promptly slammed the inner wooden doors. As there were only 20 seats in the tiny chapel, this meant pretty well everybody who had contributed to the restoration fund was outside trying to catch a glimpse of what was happening inside, and the disappointed crowd muttered and fumed at his rudeness. Good humour was only restored when the doll-pretty saint, her paint maquillage as carefully applied as any super-model's, was borne into the night on her newly restored throne by four stout lads, who tottered off to carry her around the parish. They were followed by at least 200 people clutching children and candles, a few reprobates clutching cigarettes and bottles of San Miguel, and several stray dogs.

When the 'treading of the bounds' was complete, mothers rushed to install their impatiently squealing kids onto the dodgems and roundabouts, while the elders settled down to some serious gossiping and drinking. Jack and Maud had walked down with their grandchildren and we were all having a great time when the music died, the dodgems bashed to a halt, and the fairy lights on the stalls lining the street flickered and waned to an orange glow. A puzzled buzz rose from the knots of merry-makers because the lights in the houses were mostly still ablaze, and the machines in the *ventas* were still beeping and clanging. *Que pasa*?

James glanced up at the power line that looped along the street, and the temporary cable clamped to it that was supplying the visiting stalls and amusements.

'Uh oh... Jack, what time do your irrigation pumps come on?'

Jack looked at his watch. 'The first bank comes on about now I'd say,' he replied. 'Why?'

James wordlessly pointed at the temporary connection, and the power line that looped away into the darkness in the direction of Jack's barn.

'Oh hell, you don't mean...?'

'Reckon so. Time to go home. The natives are restless tonight.'

&

James and Georg had finished at Rick and Joan's house. The new kitchen was a miracle of taps that produced water and hobs that heated. There wasn't a cockroach in sight, although Rick, shaken by the *tarantella* incident, had religiously put down traps in every cabinet and corner.

When they turned up at Finca Tara, they were still giggling like schoolboys about their last minutes at Cielo Azul. They had been doing a final clear up and could hear Rick and Joan as they put up equipment in their new kitchen.

'Give it to me, Rick.'

'Right. Make sure it's good and stiff Joan. You never make it stiff enough.'

brbrrbrrr... 'It needs to be deeper than that Rick...'

brrrrrbr ...'It's still not deep enough.'

brbrrrrrrrrrrrrrr ... 'I'm doing my best Joan.'

bbrrbbbrrrrrrbb 'Harder, Rick, *harder.*' *brbrbrrrrrrr*

Unfortunately, the boys had been so hysterical with laughter that they had had to creep out without hearing whether there was a successful outcome to Rick's hole-drilling and Joan's attempts to mix the filler.

&

Georg and James had tendered for the contract to build Don's tower, but it had gone to another company, which was disappointing, as we had all put many hours into the drawings and costing. Don had a smaller job for James, wiring up a guest bungalow in the garden. This was easy enough, except that he was shadowed by Lady Macbeth who, at any electrical *moment critique,* would demand to know, 'Who *are* you, boy?' He found this quite disturbing, not because it was distracting, but because it made him ask himself the same question.

One afternoon when they had finished work, Georg asked James whether he could help a friend with a problem generator, and suggested we all go there that evening. Karl and his wife lived on top of the 'pretty cottage' mountain and Georg drove us up there, past the cottage and the threshing floor, until we were on the flat top of the mountain, with only planes on their flight path to Malaga Airport above us. Karl and Helga didn't have the luxury of mains water or electricity, telephone or even a road to their little stone house, squatting amongst the heather and coarse grasses. They had been farming in a small way but according to Georg, their horse had dropped dead and they had just shot their last pig, so it was difficult to say what they were living on. I was interested to know why they had shot the pig rather than slaughtering it, but somehow it seemed indelicate to ask. The old car engine – which served as a generator to power their radio and a few bulbs in the kitchen and living room – was on its last legs, but James did what he could.

Kurt brought out a bottle of excellent riesling, closely followed by five more as we got into the swing of things. He then drove his WW2 *panzer wagen* onto the porch, the generator not being up to powering a cassette player, so that we could listen to his extensive collection of Irish folk music. We had rushed from home without eating anything, thinking it was going to be a brief visit, so when Helga brought out some extremely tasty pâté and *wurst* sent from Germany, we ate hungrily and with relish. Karl and Helga didn't seem in the least depressed by their lack of agricultural success and we had a wonderful evening of laughter and reminiscence.

As we left, I felt guilty that we had devoured all their wonderful food and made some apology. Kurt laughed hugely, his luxuriant moustaches whiffling. 'Ya, it's true, ve don't have much...' he looked out at the empty paddock and the abandoned pigsties. 'But ve mountain krauts like to enjoy ourselves... eating und drinking mit friends, that's the best tink in life.'

Georg hurtled back down the track with the confident

histrionics of a rally driver. His lights were courtesy of Joe Lucas (popularly known in the motor trade as 'The Prince of Darkness'), so we only saw the barest hint of the rocks that marked the edge of the track and the black void beyond, for which I was grateful. I was still feeling bad about scarfing Karl's precious supplies, wondering whether they would have anything to eat the next day, but Georg just laughed. 'Don't stress about it, it's nothing like as bad as you think. Kurt's father owns a successful shipyard, but Kurt doesn't see eye to eye with the old man. He went to University and then just dropped out, and his father was incandescent. But you've just enjoyed one of the little parcels his mama sends them! Do you feel like having a coffee and a nightcap?'

We said yes to coffee and Georg pulled up in front of a bar in Torre Alqueria. Our good intentions received a setback when we walked in and saw Antonio Manuel, José and Paco sitting plotting at a table. They wouldn't let us go without a drink or three and it was a long evening. We returned home to some hard looks from unfed cats who didn't appreciate two drunk and noisy people waking them at three o'clock in the morning for a cuddle.

On the whole animals are incredibly forgiving. The only creature I've known to bear a grudge was a racehorse which was regularly terrorised by a male groom wielding a pitchfork. The horse ended up kicking the groom in the head and, from that day on, wouldn't tolerate the presence of any man in the loosebox. This was somewhat inconvenient in a racing stable, so the owner sent the horse for training to my mother, who had a reputation for coping with tricky cases. My mother and I had no problems with the mare, to such an extent that after a year or so, we totally forgot about the grudge, and when my mother and I both had to be away the same day, my father was deputised to feed and muck out. He remembered going into the stable, but the rest was just a blur as he hurdled the stable door with the assistance of two well-placed hooves.

With the foregoing in mind, I'd hesitate to say that a cat could hold a grudge, but two days later we had a buffet lunch to return the hospitality of all our friends and neighbours. Though I still had a headache from the mountain kraut evening and didn't feel 100 percent, I carefully swept, polished and dusted the house.

As we all sat eating lunch, I noticed that Jack kept peering with a quizzical expression into a corner, but I couldn't see what he was looking at as my glasses had gone missing again. Later, when everyone had gone, I remembered his slightly odd behaviour and went to have a look – lying there in full view was a large partially-eaten rat.

Jack must have been unsure what he had actually seen as we soon received a summons to go up to La Esperanza for a chat. I hadn't been working there for some weeks because his whole family was over from England. Though she loved them dearly it was hard work for Maud, who wasn't entirely well. Jack also loved his family, but he'd become grumpy and would retire to his workshop when things got too much for him, and he was in one of his funny moods when we turned up. What he had to say came as quite a shock.

9.
A Death, and a Life

W e trooped in, wondering what Jack's mysterious summons
was about.

'Sit down James, Alex,' Jack said as he settled himself on
the sofa opposite. 'Maudie, let's have a cup of coffee.'

'I'll give Maud a hand,' I said.

'No, you stay here Alex. What I've got to say concerns both
of you.'

James and I glanced at each other, puzzled and paranoid.
What had we done, or not done?

'Hrrumph. Well, you know Maudie hasn't been too well
lately and she's finding things a bit of a strain with the family
staying. Not as young as she was.'

He was wise to say this while Maud was out of the room;
she hated to be reminded that she was older than her husband.

'The fact is, we could do with a bit more help about the
place. Catering, running the house, that sort of thing... of
course, we'd keep on the daily from the village. James, I'd want
you to keep the machinery serviced, see to any maintenance, but
you could carry on with your outside work as long as I had first
call on your time...and we'd want you to live in. The bungalow
is all set up with repeaters for the gate video, telephone,
emergency call, the lot. You could always let your place if you
didn't want to sell.'

Maud came in with the coffee tray. 'The bungalow's quite
nice Alex. Have you seen inside it? It needs a bit of tidying up
and it isn't very big of course – our first house wasn't any bigger
though, was it love?' She handed Jack his cup.

We sat, mute, stunned. Whatever we had thought Jack was
going to say, this wasn't it.

'You don't have to make a decision now. We'll be going
back to England for a few weeks anyway. Talk it over. Go down
and have a look at the bungalow; maybe you can decorate it
Alex, and it'll need painting whatever you decide to do.'

'Okay, yes, fine, Jack... we'll talk about it, thanks for the
offer,' James said. 'There's a lot to think about.'

Something about his tone alerted me to the fact that his first reaction was negative, as was mine. We had struggled and sacrificed quite a lot to become our own masters and the thought of becoming employees on 24-hour call – for we had no illusions about what would happen to our privacy – wasn't altogether appealing.

On the one hand, it would solve a lot of pressing problems. Our financial situation had improved recently, as James was earning good money, and the guests were bringing in a steady if unspectacular amount. But, we were paying off a large mortgage, and at the end of the month there was nothing left in the kitty. We were running fast, but getting nowhere, and there wasn't a rainy day fund.

On the other hand, there were interesting possibilities on the drawing board. La Cabra was being discovered and the golf course would ensure even more people became interested; we knew a couple of entrepreneurs who were combing the area for plots suitable for development. Not only would there be work for James, there was also the opportunity to earn commission for finding building plots and other spin-offs. I'd been asked to do some preliminary plans and drawings for a promotional brochure by Murray Figgis, who owned Hacyenda Lopez, a large and unusual *cortijo* next to the proposed golf course.

Hacyenda Lopez was a large, low, octagonal building with a lovely internal courtyard studded with terracotta pots of fern and geraniums. The central fountain splashing onto creamy paving stones, making a pleasing backdrop for a meal or drinks. Murray was a smooth, good-looking guy from Nottingham, and he and his young wife Pixie, having made a snap decision to live in Spain, were looking for ways to make money. Hacyenda was big enough to divide into three apartments, one of which Murray let to Georg, but Murray had seen the opportunity to make money on a much grander scale with his land, which was extensive enough to parcel into 18 building plots. The houses would be small, identical and crowded together in the English fashion, and there was a certain amount of dissatisfaction, both from the expats who were trying to rise above that sort of thing and the locals who preferred their own architecture. However, it seemed that Murray had his permissions so we would have to put up with it.

৵

Jack was thinking of giving up his commercial mandarin growing due to the falling market price and rising costs. The question of irrigation, which was essential for a good crop, was the main concern. He relied on his own boreholes for water, but one of the three was failing; Jack sent for the drill rig to sink a new one. The crew sank a test bore in a likely spot, deeper than ever before, but found nothing more than a trickle. They had a worrying tale to tell: the water table was falling quite fast, and the golf course directly opposite La Esperanza would use anything up to a million gallons a day, depleting it even more. Local mains water was expensive and metered, and was quite often turned off for many hours a day or even days at a time, so wasn't an option. Rick and Joan were on the end of the line for the water main and their pressure was so feeble they'd been coming to us for baths for the past week, and were thinking of putting in a high-level storage tank to provide extra capacity and better pressure.

Abandoning the mandarins would mean Jack had a lot of spare land, land which was within the urban planning area. James spent a morning in the planning office sounding them out and made a proposal to Jack about building a small number of quality houses on the mandarin orchard. But whichever way it went, Jack would need the water.

The drilling rig was still at La Esperanza five days later, still looking for water. Everybody was keeping a low profile while the boss raged, complaining about the shortcomings of his employees and the uselessness of the rig, despite their high-tech ground-mapping techniques. He would have sacked them if it hadn't been essential to sink another bore. But then the remaining estate worker, Ramon Gonzalez, had a brainwave: his old dad was a dowser, so why didn't Jack let him have a go at finding water?

Jack didn't really believe in that sort of thing, but he was so desperate that anything was worth a try, and Ramon summoned his father.

The old boy turned up clutching the tools of his trade – a pendulum and a metal coat hanger – and after a keen look at the lie of the land, started walking the estate. He seemed attracted to a particular area and, after a while, became quite animated as the pendulum picked up momentum.

'*Aqui*, *Señor*... here is your water, much water, and not too deep!'

We all clustered around, fascinated. The riggers weren't quite so thrilled, having already surveyed this area and found nothing, but work was work, so they grumpily drove the rig over and positioned the drill bit exactly over the spot indicated by Gonzalez *père*.

❧

The big drill bit into the ground and the cooling, lubricating mud started flowing, shortly followed by an enormous geyser of clear water that had us leaping backwards; no one had expected results this quickly. The head rigger stopped the drill and withdrew it. Ignoring the deluge, the men enlarged the hole with mattocks and peered into it. They straightened up, shouting and gesticulating, so we all crowded around and peered in too, to see a neatly-punctured, iron mains pipe.

The driver backed the heavy rig away from the rapidly flooding area in such a hurry that he didn't notice the rectangular patch of concrete with a manhole cover in it behind the lorry. There was a crunching noise as the manhole cover caved in, revealing the cesspit underneath.

'Get off, get off quick!' Ramon yelled, windmilling his arms.

The rig driver lurched forward onto the drive, more

interested in what was happening in his rear-view mirror than what was in front of him. He hadn't gone more than five feet when the offside front wheel rolled into the open inspection pit where James had been working on the gate electrics, and the rig came to a halt at a strange angle. The driver revved frantically, producing clouds of black smoke, but no movement: the rig was stuck fast. He switched off the engine.

A thick silence fell, broken only by the rush and patter of the arching water in the background. We stood silent, with our heads diplomatically lowered, watching Jack out of the corners of our eyes.

Surprisingly, he strode away towards the house, returning with a bottle of Glenfiddich and shot glasses, giving everybody a hefty slug.

The head rigger smacked his lips. His mud-caked hand shot out and plucked the bottle out of Jack's fist. '*Eh, tan bueno wicky, caballero,*' he pronounced. 'It's not bad.' He peered at the label before inserting the bottle in his mouth and taking a long gulp. 'Not as good a drink as Tres Sietes (a popular, cheap Spanish brandy), but I'll buy a couple of bottles off you if they aren't too expensive.'

Jack growled menacingly. The rigger had gone too far and a volcanic explosion was inevitable.

Ramon looked at James and James looked at me. To stay would be in the same bad taste as gawping at a fatal traffic accident. Silently we crept away through the oleanders, suppressing the odd hiccup.

~

The weather broke and the Costa del Sol abruptly went from having too little water to having a great deal too much. The storm lasted twelve hours as the thunder reverberated around the hills, deafening and unremitting, as if some terrible celestial battle was being fought above our heads. Then the rain speared down and we crouched indoors unable to think or do anything useful.

As in the previous year, the storm caused a huge amount of damage and several people lost their lives. We also suffered a loss, small in the great scheme of things, but distressing to us.

After the storm, the cats went outside – we'd shut them in because we didn't want a repeat of last year's incident with Smoo – and they shot off on their mysterious rounds. I glimpsed Luigi once, far away on the hillside opposite, picking his way across a ploughed field. It wasn't the first time I'd seen him there, but it was to be the last. About mid-morning, I heard a lot of barking and saw a couple of men with guns and their pack of hunting dogs which lived about a mile away in the next valley. When Luigi didn't return, we searched until dark, calling and calling, but in my heart I knew what had happened to my endlessly curious little cat.

The weather continued to be unpleasant, with heavy grey clouds and high humidity, until we had another storm a couple of weeks later. We had gone down to Fuengirola so that James could do a small plumbing job for Freddie, who was in remission and mobile again. Afterwards we went to visit a friend, who welcomed us into her house with apologies for the mess of towels and eyedroppers lying around.

'It's a war zone in here,' she said, booting her yowling Siamese cat out of the room and showing us a tiny, ugly black and white kitten lying in a shoebox. 'I found this dying on the riverbank after the big storm – I didn't know what to do.... I mean could *you* have just left it? But the trouble is Daisy just loathes it and she's *soo* spiteful, I can see *big* trouble ahead. It never stops demanding milk and I have to work, there's no way I can keep it... have you seen my *garden*?... *one* locust did that, completely stripped the whole garden. Can you *imagine* what it must be like in Africa?'

I tried to listen to the stream-of-consciousness conversation and ignore the ugly kitten with its bent, ricketty legs and starvation belly. James shook his head warningly, but it was no good – it reminded me so much of Luigi; the markings were similar though it had none of his neat beauty. But there was a cat-shaped hole in our household and this vaguely cat-shaped blob needed a home. The eyedropper and milk went into a bag and we were on our way, with Ugly lying on a towel in my lap purring so loudly he could be heard over the noise of the engine, his microscopic claws treadling like mad. He knew he'd found a home and now the only problem was going to be persuading Smoo that he needed a kitten in his life.

Food is always a good start, so I put down a bowl of cat food for Smoo before introducing the stranger. The kitten jerked itself out of my hands and flubbed across the tiles, its distended belly almost on the ground. It launched itself headfirst into senior cat's bowl, where it latched onto a chunk of meat half its size and started gulping voraciously. Smoo looked at it with loathing and stalked out. As James tried to prise it off the meat, it sank its tiny fangs in his thumb and started chewing – Muppet, as we called him, had come to stay and he didn't intend to go hungry. Smoo hated Muppet – which was good in a way as he'd been pining for Luigi and not eating; now he ate to clear his dish before Muppet clambered in and started hoovering. The milk dropper was ditched as an unnecessary affectation.

Coping with a kitten which thought it was a starving Rottweiler took my mind off my own troubles. For some time I'd been suffering from what is known in delicate circles as female problems, and a visit to a Malaga specialist had indicated that an operation was needed, sooner rather than later. A Gibraltarian doctor I'd known for many years advised me that the best option – since I qualified to enter the Naval Hospital – was to have the operation in Gibraltar; and so he arranged it.

I was overcome by dark thoughts as I left Finca Tara, especially when we passed under the banana palms that we'd planted near the front door. Local people came to look at them as they didn't normally grow at our altitude, but would I be around to see the green bananas turn yellow? Would we be able to cope financially? I wouldn't be able to lift anything – not even a kettle – for six weeks, and would need three months off work. Eileen, a dear friend for many years since we'd lived next door to each other in London had offered to come and help me in the immediate post-operative period, and I was looking forward to seeing her. Her common sense and cooking skills were legendary, and her obsession with a clean and tidy house wouldn't go amiss either, since the battle with constant pain meant I hadn't been doing much housework.

The Naval Hospital hadn't changed a great deal since the Battle of Trafalgar. The tall-ceilinged, airy wards with mosquito nets hooked on the wall over each bed would have seemed familiar enough to Lord Nelson. So would the naval discipline observed by the medical orderlies and the corridors painted a stomach-churning combination of chocolate and bile green.

The pre-med given, I kissed my husband goodbye, surprised to see him red-eyed and twitchy. Things had been so difficult over the past months that we had been growing apart, and I knew he was nearing the end of his tether with my whey-faced depression and need for days in bed.

'Don't worry old thing,' I whispered, 'the surgeon promised I'd be better than new when she's finished with me.'

'Better get back to the pussies before Muppet gets shreddled then. Good luck.' He kissed my cheek and walked away, his tall lean figure dwindling into the distance between the regimentally-spaced beds.

Two smiling orderlies appeared, saucy in their smart white tropical kit, and I smiled back, wondering if all the female patients fancied them.

'You all set to go down to theatre Miss?' the older one asked.

'Ready as I'll ever be...'

They wheeled the gurney alongside, then '*Hup*, two, six!' and we were rolling.

'What's the 'two six' routine?' I asked drowsily.

'Goes back to when we had horses pulling the gun carriages, Miss,' one of them replied. 'If there were other duties, horses number two and six were detached to do them.'

'So you two are horses two and six then?'

'Yes, Miss.'

'You're in the right place if you get a stone in your hoof then...' It was a pathetically feeble joke, but we found it pretty funny, and the theatre staff looked taken aback as we pushed through the swing doors hooting with laughter.

'We don't get many patients coming in here laughing,' commented the anaesthetist as he slid the needle into a vein.

'They would if they knew that you're all horses,' I slurred, and was still giggling as I slid into unconsciousness under the anaesthetist's puzzled frown.

It wasn't quite so funny coming round again, but it was certainly a relief to have little pain; in fact, it was so bearable and the dressing so minuscule that I peeked under the dressing and had a real panic attack to discover that there didn't seem to be any stitches either. I thought maybe the surgeon had cancelled the operation and called the nurse in a panic, but she reassured me that they sometimes did internal stitching that was naturally absorbed by the body. A big plus if there were no stitches to come out.

Someone had given me the excellent advice to have nothing but fluids for the 48 hours before the operation, so I had none of the painful gas that afflicts most abdominal post-ops and was out of bed and walking in record time, thankful to avoid having a bedpan delivered by a cherubic youth in tight white shorts and black hobnailed boots.

There was a second shock in Ablutions when faced with a naked matelot stepping out of the shower: it wasn't so much his nakedness, as the fact that he had a pelt of curly black hair over his entire body. I couldn't help wondering what they would do if he ever caught crabs. He was embarrassed and apologised profusely. Matron usually managed to keep the men one end of the mixed ward and the women the other end, and we avoided using the 'the other end's' facilities, but his Glaswegian shipmates had brought him a liquid present and he admitted to being 'Just a wee bit off me haed.'

The surgeon came in to tell me that the operation had been long but had gone well. She leaned on her walking stick as she explained that they had caught the cancer in time – I could go home with a tranquil mind and wouldn't have any more pain. Her tired smile and stick hinted that she knew a bit about pain.

The hospital discharged me three days early, and Paddy drove me home to Finca Tara. The bananas still weren't ripe, Smoo still hated Muppet and the house was full of flowers, cards and visitors. My husband hugged me and suddenly the world seemed a sunnier place.

10.
Recovery

Hospital horror stories were all the rage. Freddie was in the hospital for another bout of chemotherapy and Nigel to have the hardware in his leg removed. He'd had a nasty accident three months previously, when he lost his balance strimming a steep bank and tumbled down the slope, smashing his femur in several places when he rolled under the car at the bottom. It was the sort of break requiring an operation to patch the bone together with plates and pins. The surgeon had muttered about amputation as a last resort and they'd had a couple of weeks of hell until it became clear that the pinning operation was a success and the spectre of disability receded.

The few hale and hearty La Cabrans left spent a lot of time in the following weeks visiting the halt and the lame, but gradually we all got back on our feet again and returned to normal. Antonio came over the track with some veggies and a pot of geraniums when he saw me shuffling around the garden, wishing I could get at weeds that appeared to have grown at least a foot in my absence.

'*Eeuhh,* so how was it, the operation?'

'Fine, absolutely fine, *no problema* thank you, Antonio.' I was surprised he even knew about it – I hadn't said anything and I very much doubted that James had either.

'And the scar, how big is that?'

I bridled slightly. This was the sort of question one expected from female friends, not a bachelor Spanish *campesino.* 'Er, well, *regular,* Antonio. Umm, *normal.*'

'My cousin Carmen, she had a scar from here to here.' Antonio indicated that she had been virtually cut in half. 'And it looked like a *tiburon,* a shark, had bitten her, all red and jagged.' He looked expectantly at my stomach, obviously hoping that something even more thrilling than a shark bite was going to be revealed. 'And then she got an infection with pus...'

'No, nothing like that,' I muttered, suddenly feeling faint. 'How's your father?' I'd been hoping to distract Antonio's attention, but it wasn't the right question.

'*Eeuuh, el pobrecito* ... he wasn't able to pee, in terrible pain because he was full of water you see, swelling up, and I had to take him to hospital in the middle of the night.'

I tutted. 'He's alright now?' It was another bum question.

'*Si, si, claro*...but they had to put the umbrella up him.'

'The *what*?' It was the stupidest question yet, but I had to know.

'The umbrella... the doctor put a metal umbrella up his penis, folded of course, then opened it and pulled it down, several times over. My father was screaming with pain, but it has to be done.' Antonio mimed the movement and shrugged nonchalantly as a man of the world, familiar with all things gynaecological, male or female.

I made my excuses and wobbled indoors for a nice lie down while Eileen made me a cup of tea; it had been more wracking than any hospital soap.

We went to Venta Moreno for a little celebration, only to find it packed with a wedding party, but they fitted us in somehow. It was the usual thing: dozens of small children in their party clothes playing among the tables, while their elders made endless toasts to the bride and groom, and everybody was fairly merry. The bride's mother stood and made a little speech, reminding the groom of his duties towards her daughter. She beckoned to the waiter, who brought a covered silver salver to the table, placing it in front of the groom. Whipping the cover off the waiter stepped back with a grin. On the salver was a huge carrot flanked by two hardboiled eggs. The wedding party dissolved into screams of laughter. It only lacked Paco to give us one of his comments on the human condition.

Finca Tara was expecting some paying guests and, as usual, the resident wildlife was playing its downright awkward part. The kitchen had been given its normal thorough clean before guests arrived, but despite using a good strong pine-scented cleaner there was a persistent unpleasant smell; not drains, rotting food or cat faeces, but something in between, and as bad as all three. The finger of suspicion, as usual, pointed at Muppet, who seemed to spend an unnatural proportion of his day lurking under the kitchen cabinets.

We had to do something. In desperation, James pulled out all the cabinets and behind the dishwasher we saw two black beetles with large shiny elytrons curving to a point at the rear end. They looked suspiciously like cockroaches, but didn't scuttle away when exposed to the light, so we were about to dismiss them as irrelevant when Muppet pounced, trying to tip one over. There was a loud pop followed by a vile smell and Muppet reached for the other beetle with an exploratory talon. A pop came from the second beetle's rear end and we coughed as another mephitic cloud drifted under our noses.

We had certainly found the source of the bad smell and it was, as suspected, all Muppet's fault. The bug book my parents had given us for Christmas identified them as *Blaps mucronata*, the Churchyard beetle. Muppet was fortunate they weren't the similar Bombardier beetle, or he might have got an explosion of boiling liquid in his face rather than just a bad smell. These unique creatures have a fireproof chamber in their backsides and, when annoyed, they combine hydrogen peroxide and hydroquinone, stored separately in the abdomen – which instantly explodes. The Bombardier can direct the resulting 212°F (100°C) irritant wet fart with devastating accuracy in any direction at 500 pulses a second. This earns it respect from both predators and scientists, who cannot believe such a schoolboys' dream could evolve naturally.

On the day of the guests' arrival, there was a prolonged downpour, punctuated by the arrival of a caravan of wet, irritable, tired and emotional people. First Georg and Amado – his Spanish sidekick – shouldered their way through the door. Closely followed by the guests, their taxi driver and a mound of luggage, followed by Murray and Pixie, who were extremely drunk and waving bottles, followed by their dog, followed by James. The dining hall suddenly seemed very damp and full as everybody started complaining or explaining at once.

'That taxi driver is *un hombre sin verguenza,* shameless, Alex...,'

'Are you Mrs Browning? We were supposed to be met at the airport...'

'*Buenas tardes Señora,* a place of such impossibility to find...

'Yoo hoo Alex, let's have a little drinkie!'

'God, I'm sorry, but Arrivals was packed...'

The threads were gradually un-entwined: James had gone to the airport to pick up the guests, but due to the arrival hall being full of scaffolding and confused passengers, had missed them.

The guests had taken a taxi, but the driver didn't understand English or the map we provided or the address, and they had toured a large part of Andalucia before stopping at the Goat and Garlic to ask the way.

The barman at the Goat and Garlic confused them totally by saying: 'Si, si, you want Mr James,' to which they replied 'No, no, we want Mr Browning,' which totally confused the barman, who didn't know our surname. Things then got a bit heated; the taxi driver, who wasn't enjoying his trip into the *campo*, was saying rude things to the barman about *guiris* who didn't know their arse from their elbow. The barman, who knew many of his *guiri* customers understood Spanish, was diplomatically telling him to shut up, and the guests were moaning that no one understood them in this god-forsaken dump. Georg, who was having a drink at the bar with Amado, was highly amused by this inter-cultural fracas until the penny dropped as to who they were. He could see there was a distinct possibility that they would shortly be seeing the rest of Andalucia, so offered to show the taxi driver the way to the *finca*.

Murray and Pixie were feeling like company after a liquid lunch, so they had joined the procession wending its way towards Finca Tara. They all arrived at once and Georg and the taxi driver had a row about the fare as the guests had asked him to intervene on their behalf, while Murray and Pixie waved bottles and giggled a lot.

Our guests looked in bewilderment at the heaving mass in the hallway.

'Are they all staying here?' asked the lady guest in a slightly apprehensive tone, flinching as Pixie's large, wet dog thrust his nose into her groin. Amado, less than fragrant in his vilest working clothes, had just accepted a large drink from one of Murray's bottles, and Pixie had draped herself around James's neck, looking languorously into his eyes. Georg, on behalf of our guests, had finally succeeded in beating down the taxi driver's extortionate demands; generous in victory, the Austrian embraced him and handed him a glass of wine.

The chaotic scene looked cheerily alpine thanks to the white flakes of paint drifting down from the ceiling – it had been a mistake using plastic paint over whitewash because damp weather always caused a violent reaction.

'No, don't worry,' I said. 'None of them will be staying. I'm so sorry my husband missed you at the airport, it's a bit of a problem while they're altering the arrivals hall. Would you like to see your room or would you prefer a drink?'

Chauffeured trips to local places of interest were offered for guests who didn't want to hire a car and drive themselves, and Malaga city is well worth a tour. I took them to the Gibralfaro, a Moorish fort on a crag overlooking the city and the harbour. It's quite a steep climb up the decorative brick steps and I was puffing and panting and almost ready to give up when we met two frail, elderly Americans coming down, one of them using two sticks. Strangely, I was then able to get to the top, where we found a magnificent view over the harbour and an abandoned fridge. After that, I wasn't quite so sure that I'd made such a wonderful recovery from the operation, but it was obviously an effortless climb for most of the population, with or without surplus white goods. Once back in town, we hired a carriage for a sightseeing tour of the old city. The driver enquired whether we wanted a fast tour or a slow tour, as Marguerite had only two paces. Out of sisterly consideration for the elderly horse, I opted for the slow version, which allowed a thorough appreciation of the architectural pleasures of the city and the wonderful botanical gardens.

Our guests turned out to be good sports, seeing the funny side of being stuck for a week in a damp, draughty, cat-and-beetle-infested madhouse; fortunately, they enjoyed assessing the relative merits of the many Spanish wine regions. Their entry in the visitor's book read: *'It isn't like being on holiday... it's just like coming home every evening.'* I felt sorry for them when I read that – they must have led a stressful life.

Georg and James were in good spirits as they had signed a contract to build a house for Joe, a Marbella-based businessman. Joe was married to a distant relative of mine and when they came to La Cabra for lunch to see our house, Joe liked what he saw of the neighbourhood and decided to invest some money in property development. The boys felt that the contract called for a celebration and we planned to go to a nightclub in Malaga that Georg liked.

A *Romería (*a pilgrimage involving a religious image transported by wagon, accompanied by a retinue of riders) was taking place in the district or *barrio,* and James and I meandered for a while, looking at the desirable horses and their equally desirable riders. The lean, dark-eyed men looked impossibly romantic in their traditional *traje Andaluz* of tight striped trousers, waistcoat over ruffled white shirt, suede boots and, in some cases, a black pillbox hat tipped at a jaunty angle over the brow. The girls mounted behind their beaus fanned themselves or carefully spread their cascading skirts over the horses' flanks. The screams of laughter and preening chatter, the lustrous hair studded with jewels and flowers, made one think of an aviary of exotic birds. Children dressed like miniature adults rode proudly alongside their parents, to the admiring exclamations of the crowd.

Many of the male riders preferred sitting in a bar to sitting on their horses, and every lamp post had at least one animal with its reins looped over the 'No Waiting' sign. Unlike Pogo, the horses behaved perfectly, even blood stallions standing like statues while the crowd swirled around them. Every now and again, the police would make an effort to clear the street so the traffic could get through; the riders who were hauled out of bars mounted their horses, but instead of moving off they used whip and spur to make them dance and curvet while the dodging officers cursed and threatened. The crowd was highly amused by these tactics, which infuriated the officers even more, and when they radioed for reinforcements the riders admitted defeat and the whole cavalcade swung into action. They clattered off down the street after the ox cart bearing the statue of the Virgin, the horses arching their necks and tossing their flowing manes, glad to be finally on the move.

The nightclub where we were meeting Georg was in full swing as the dancers, some in designer jeans and others in traditional dress, swirled and clapped, clacking castanets and throwing their partners smouldering glances in the traditional *Sevillana* gypsy dance.

'*Aquí* James, over here!' Georg shouted over the hubbub.

'You've just missed a fab flamenco competition,' burbled Pixie. 'Georg and his girlfriend had a go. It was an absolute scream, they did ever so well.'

'What do you want to drink?' asked Georg, seeing the waiter struggling through the packed dancers.

I wriggled onto the seat next to Pixie. 'The dancing looks fun, but you won't get me up there, I haven't the faintest idea how to dance a *Sevillana*,' I said.

'Ooh, you must come to the classes they're starting in the village then, Murray and I have just signed up for the six-week course, it'll be fantastic if we all do it.' Pixie tapped her empty glass. 'Where's the waiter? I'm parched...Oh there he is at

▲ *Pogo & Alex competing*

▼ *The well-house*

▲ *A shady spot*

▶ *Luigi*

▲ *Quicksilver microlight*

▼ *Billy Goat*

▼ *Smoo & Houdini in
Carpenter-bee bower*

▼ *Traudle's goat
gives birth*

▼ *Ancient olive tree*

▶ *Muppet looking for trouble*

▼ *Finca Tara*

▶ *Mule with portable plough*

▼ *Antonio ploughing his* **huerta**

◄
James at La Herradura

▼ *The railway road
after the storm*

▲ *James, the Captain, Alex, Hope*

▼ *Enjoying the view*

last…It's a miracle they don't pour the drinks over everybody in this scrum,' she remarked.

The waiter, with tray held triumphantly aloft, reached our table, where he tripped over Pixie's bulging handbag and lunged forward with a shout of dismay. The drinks flew into the air to shower down, every drop spattering over Pixie and I. It was such a coincidence that we burst into howls of laughter and the more the waiter apologised and mopped at us, the more hysterical we got, while the rest of the party looked on in puzzlement. It was late before we got home, tired and sticky, but fired up with the notion of learning to dance the *Sevillana*.

We heard next day that Georg and Evyllin, his Santa Dominguin girlfriend, had crashed on their way home. A tyre burst and Georg's rallying technique wasn't good enough to stop the BMW veering across the road and demolishing a Fiesta, before falling into a ditch. The car was a write-off and Evyllin had a broken collarbone, which put Georg in a rather awkward position, as he had been enjoying an emotionally uncommitted relationship with the gorgeous pouting girl. She, however, had a quite different agenda. Georg felt obliged to invite her to move into Hacyenda Lopez so he could look after her on a temporary basis – not too long afterwards the word was that he was going to Santa Domingo to meet Evyllin's family.

The La Cabra Cultural Centre was a grand name for a large room that housed various activities and classes. James and I were surprised to find how many people had turned up for the beginners' *Sevillana* class; mostly foreigners, of course, as Spanish children learn their traditional dances at an early age and are expert by the time they're teenagers. There's no whiff of amused contempt about it, no sniggering about Morris dancers and bells and hankies – they love to dance and the old dances are fun, at least they are to the Spanish, who, if they're too infirm to whirl around the floor, can join in with the intricate clapping that's part of the dance.

The teacher divided us into groups and demonstrated the

various steps, which looked easy enough. Except that you have to include body, arm and hand movements, toss your hair, cast smouldering glances at the opposite sex, watch your deportment, hold your clothes just so, suck your stomach in, stamp your feet and be aware what everybody else is doing at the same time. It's exhausting and depressing when you realise that you have the timing and co-ordination of a socially-challenged crab missing a couple of legs. The only consolation for most of us was that Traudl was worse, consistently whirling in the wrong direction like a malignant spinning top, knocking neighbouring dancers disastrously off course as they ducked under her flailing arms. After three or four lessons, we were sort of getting the hang of it and working up to speed; poor Traudl, however, didn't seem to improve at all. She skittled more people to the floor as she tried to go faster and the teacher attempted, with the greatest tact, to persuade her not to come any more. But, Traudl enjoyed the company, so we had to learn to live with it.

☙

The local tip was a spectre in our lives that we were constantly aware of, much as those who live in the shadow of an active volcano must be aware. Although it was a couple of miles away and hidden behind a belt of trees, we could tell its state by the pall of smoke that hung over it, or, given the wind in our direction, by the stink or the sound of the caterpillar tractor pushing the rubbish into a steep ravine. The stream which somehow managed to creep and seep its way through the ravine and on through the orchards, fields, gardens and farms to the sea, carried with it all the noxious chemicals that batteries, oil, chemical residues, paints and rotting carcasses could impart. Arsenic, chlorine, isocyanates, lead, mercury, nitrates, nitrites and terpenes all leached out of the mountain of rotting waste by the stream and trickled atom by atom into wells and drinking water.

We were lucky that it didn't affect our aquifer, but I

wondered how many people and animals downstream suffered mystery illnesses? It was undeniably handy to have a tip, as you could dump anything without needing permission: diseased carcasses from the slaughterhouse, dead goats and horses, stinking fish and rotting fruit and vegetables all made a regular appearance. Razor-ribbed, feral dogs and massive fuliginous pigs wavered like wraiths in the heat-hazed air. A couple of tin shacks stood slack-hipped at the festering rubbish-strewn entrance, like ticket booths to Hades. They were the dwellings of the tip hounds – small, dark men with red-rimmed eyes who combed the dross for treasures to sell at the Fuengirola flea market.

James took the rubbish there one evening while I was staying up at Freddie and Felicity's new house on the *camino forestal* (logging road through a forest) overlooking Alhaurin el Grande. I was looking after Scruffy overnight while his owners were at the hospital, so I didn't know what had happened until Penny drove up to the cottage and told me that my husband had hurt himself. James had slipped and gone down on his knee, straight onto a shard of broken glass which was so sharp that he didn't realise what had happened until blood started gushing down his leg. He bound it as tight as possible and, in agonising pain, managed to drive into Alhaurin el Grande to the *ambulatorio* (walk-in clinic) where he found a long line of elderly Spanish ladies waiting to see the female doctor.

The old ladies took one look at the *guiri's* deathly pale face and the blood trickling over his boot, and knocked on the doctor's door, hauling out the indignant incumbent in mid-complaint and thrusting James in. The doctor neatly cut the leg off his best work trousers to see what the damage was, but decided it was too much of a job for her – James would have to go to Malaga hospital. James called Nigel on the radiophone and Nigel drove him to the hospital that he knew so well, having been there for his broken leg. Nigel went to look for the surgeon who had pinned him together, and found him in the hospital bar in black leather biker gear, chatting up the nurses before leaving for the evening. Nigel persuaded him to return to A & E, where the surgeon removed the glass dagger and put in nine stitches, tut tutting at the damage.

I'd been waiting at Nigel and Penny's place for them to return, so nervous that I'd sailed through Penny's monumental pile of ironing without thinking about it, a job I usually hate.

James was more annoyed about his ruined trousers than anything, although having to be off work for a week didn't please him either. Poor man, he'd had his 40th birthday earlier that week and not a very happy one at that, as the difficult patch we'd been going through for some months ended in a row about the lack of birthday preparations on my part. We didn't normally fight and I now felt sick and guilty every time I thought about what could have happened if he'd hit an artery – the feral pigs and the dogs wouldn't have left much forensic evidence. They say that every cloud has a silver lining: this particular cloud brought me to my senses.

ఞ

The valley rang and reverberated with cuckoos calling back and forth until one longed to shoot them. They're horrid, dull birds despite their undeserved popularity as a sign of spring. The bee-eaters – little jewel-feathered birds that live in sandy banks – and the striking black-crested hoopoes, with their strange looping flight and 'hoop hoop' call are far more welcome; even the hoopoe's Latin name, *Upupa epops,* makes one smile. Although we weren't on the main passerine migration route – which passes over Gibraltar – the spring brought a flood of bird sightings and sounds, a waterfall of song every morning that promised warmer weather to come.

It wasn't only the weather that was improving, even our financial situation was a bit easier as James had earned some commission from finding building sites. I had two apartments on the coast to decorate for friends of Don's and the guests were ticking over. It seemed like a good time to find some alternative transport to the unreliable Fiat and we found a 250cc Montesa trials bike in Alhaurin el Grande that would be manageable for me – or at least in theory. In practice, it became hard to start shortly after becoming our property and was so sharp on the clutch that I stalled it continuously, leading to slanging matches with James who had no patience with my girly problems. I omitted to tell him about the time I shot across a main road at about 60mph, missing a car by inches because I'd confused the brake with the accelerator, which would have totally wrecked our improving relationship.

The bike was named Billy Goat as it reminded me of the caprine sadist my mother kept when I was a child, which took every opportunity to butt me into the bramble bushes. This happened quite often because I was so stupid and ran round and round the tethering post rather than running away in a straight line. Billy Goat lived up to his name by wounding James's teenage daughter Vicky, who was even more hopeless as a biker than me. After stalling it a few times in tribute to her stepmother she got flustered, and when James shouted at her to give it some welly she did – dumping the clutch so suddenly the bike did a violent wheelie and leaped into the air like a Lipizzaner stallion performing airs above the ground in the Vienna Riding School. Vicky fell off over the back wheel, hurting herself quite badly, so we made James ride Billy Goat home, while we took the car. He, of course, had no problems with the bike: even machines know when to give in graciously.

11.
The Snail Men

The view from our garden of Antonio's collection of clapped-out work-horse vans and rubbish wasn't improving. Antonio had recently been forced to buy a slightly younger van to take his produce to market and to transport the big lead acid batteries he relied on for power in the house, added to which the Malaga branch of the family had donated a further example of Seat's lack of engineering finesse to the budding Motor Museum. It only needed a couple of snarling Alsatians to see him well on the way to a breaker's yard – his guard dog Pito didn't really cut the mustard as even Muppet could duff him up. Jack must have heard us whining about this blot on the landscape as, just as we were about to change to go out to supper with friends one evening, he roared up on his old grey Ferguson tractor and trailer, and dumped 27 Leylandii in the drive.

'Been sorting out my hedges and these don't match the other firs,' Jack yelled over the thumping diesel. 'They should be okay if you get 'em in straight away Alex. See you in three weeks time – Maud and I are off to England tonight.'

As the trailer vanished around the corner, the rain started pattering down. We had an hour and a half before we were due for supper – many miles away, halfway up a mountain – with people we didn't know too well.

'You and your artsy-fartsy gardening ideas,' James said, giving me a withering look as we rushed to put on our wellies.

The trees were big, about nine feet tall, too big for this sort of transplant at this time of year. Every minute the roots dried out they had less chance of surviving, but it was worth a try. The man of the family set-to digging holes like a mechanical woodpecker, the mattock whistling through the expletive-laden air, while I jammed the trees in and 'laced' them in place with whippy bamboo canes and stakes.

It wasn't long before Antonio and his father came out – with sacks over their heads against the downpour – to oversee and discuss what we were doing.

'*Oiga me*, listen, these trees are too big, they'll never

survive, will they Dad?' Antonio turned to his parent for confirmation.

'*Es verdad*, Antonio is correct, it's the wrong time of year for them, you're wasting your time,' confirmed his parent cheerfully.

The clods of mud on our boots got larger and heavier by the minute as we worked to the background music of the yelps and screams of Muppet and Pito disembowelling each other under a bush, and our neighbours dissecting our horticultural practices. It probably *was* a waste of time, but it seemed ungrateful not to try, and we carried on until all 27 trees were up and watered-in. It certainly did make a good barrier between us and Antonio, defining our new orchard pleasingly and almost hiding the horrors beyond.

We arrived for supper late – sweaty, mud-stained, embarrassingly hungry and barely speaking to each other – to find our hostess and her guests deep in discussion about classical music. She had been a concert pianist in her youth, but getting a concert grand up the side of a mountain had proved impractical and she blamed her husband for that and most of the other ills of the world. They both drank to forget – they'd forgotten what it was they needed to forget years before, but habit kept them going. They were generous hosts when it came to drink, so everyone – especially our hostess – was too pissed to care much about food. When it did finally arrive, every desiccated mouthful was followed from plate to mouth by the pleading eyes of their drooling mastiffs. Our hosts fed their dogs choice morsels – in fact the only edible bits – throughout the meal, a mediaeval habit I seemed to be alone in finding utterly repulsive. James and I returned home in much the same state as we had left it, muttering evilly and with roiling stomachs. This, after all, was the couple who heated their pool with a glass wall made of used wine bottles. It had seemed like a good cheap idea, but James and I at least agreed on one thing: we didn't have the alcoholic stamina to follow their example.

If Jack's trees were a bone of contention, the vine arbour was a great success, possibly because Antonio had donated and planted the vine sprigs. The bare sticks he had thrust into the earth a year previously had morphed into a miraculous riot of spiral tendrils snaking across the wire supports, turning almost overnight into delicately-dentillated green leaves enfolding bunches of tiny pearl-like grapes. He had given us two varieties of table grape – one black and one white – clones of the huge knotted vines that hung over his own porch. The vine arbour, which ran from the columns framing the entrance almost to the house, was long enough to provide thick shade for three or four cars and produced enough grapes to supply a hospital, or a million wasps. In our case it *was* a million wasps, which had taken up residence under the roof tiles and were a constant trial.

The entire garden had been oxen-ploughed and the garden features blocked in the previous year. The hedges, shrubs and borders had been established, but the featureless weed-pocked area marked 'lawn' on the garden plan now needed serious attention. I thought about – and dismissed – the idea of asking the Water Fairy to come and plant it with the same *grama* grass as the pool lawn. The garden lawn was four times the size of the pool lawn and would cost a fortune; we had made a lawn from scratch at Mouse Cottage so surely we could do the same here?

The syncopated clopping of hooves interrupted garden-magazine-perfect visions of velvet sward. I looked up to see a mule ambling past with a pile of wood and metal on its back, topped with a small boy like a cherry on a fairy cake. They were 100 yards away before I'd realised *what* the boy was sitting on and I belted down the track after him.

'Oy, *chico*, stop!' I panted. 'Can you plough the patch back there for me?'

The lad pulled up. '*Si, Señora, no problema, en este momento?*'

Juanito guided the mule back to the garden and let it graze

while he unloaded the pieces from the pannier boxes on its back, bolting them together to form a basic single furrow plough. Within minutes the young ploughboy was turning over the lawn area, the soil combining thin and sandy patches and ball-like clay, the worst of all worlds. The mule knew it all without the boy saying a word or pulling the reins; he knew when to pull and when to back up, when to turn and swing around the tree roots. Despite being a rather small, scrawny specimen, he had the job done in half the time it would have taken a tractor. Juanito piled the plough and shafts back into the panniers and hopped on top, and the 33-year-old mule shambled off down the track at a smart clip, the 14-year-old ploughboy well pleased with the money they'd earned that morning. It was difficult to say who was the senior partner in this working relationship but, perhaps unusually for a Spaniard, Juanito seemed to love and respect his clever old mule.

After hours of raking and levelling, I cast the seed, feeling suitably biblical dipping my hand into the apron folded around my waist and throwing each handful in a carefully regulated arc. Then I went indoors to rest, conscious of a job well done.

In the cool of the evening we strolled out to look at the velvet lawn to be.

'Are you sure you used enough seed?' said James. 'It looks a bit thin on the ground to me.'

'Shitty death, I don't BELIEVE it! I'll torch the little bastards,' I screeched. There was a fringe of bare earth totally stripped of seeds all around the outside and thick undulating boas of ants were carrying away what remained from the centre of the lawn. We bent down to examine them more closely: each ant was clasping a seed to its bosom like a hyperactive caber-tosser, millions of little tossers dashing back to the nest. The largest biomass on the planet is said to be formed by ants and the epicentre seemed to be our garden. It was warfare. I rushed around sprinkling various noxious substances on them, but they just worked faster. The ant alert was turning the writhing boas into torpid anacondas, too massive to get down their nest holes. It was becoming difficult to see any seeds at all and I began to worry about the size of the underground nests: perhaps the house would slide into a vast underground ant megalopolis?

'Don't cry dear, I'll deal with this, go and have a cup of tea,' James said, straightening his back as he headed towards the potting shed.

From the kitchen I heard a great *FATOOOM* and rushed out to see James staggering about with a dazed expression and scorched eyebrows, while flames and smoke poured from holes in the ground. The ants were vaporised. Unfortunately the ensuing firestorm didn't do the new *transparente* hedges much good either. Our victory left me feeling a bit ashamed of myself. It's difficult being a farmer or gardener and reconciling human needs and expectations with an interest in, and care for, the other inhabitants of our planet. I admit to being an ecological Jekyll and Hyde. Having damaged the hedges, it was a relief to see the *transparente* covered in fresh new leaves and Red Admiral butterflies, so many that they bowed the remaining branches to the ground.

The wildlife gets its own back sometimes – the B52 bees certainly did. Keef and Becky had built a wonderful rustic arbour over the concrete dining table in the garden, which was soon covered by a rampant pink orchidaceous bignonia smothered in blossom for most of the year. Sitting under the dappled shade for lunch or a glass of wine in the evening as we chatted about our day was a pleasure... until a deep, resonant droning signalled a Carpenter bee in an overhead holding pattern. The iridescent black bumblers liked to hover at head height, a little too close for comfort, as they examined you for dry rot. Only the females, in fact, have a sting and, being laid-back ladies, are more interested in babies than violence, so they seldom use them. But few guests were interested in the sex of the creature that appeared to be about to deliver a sting the size of a horse hypodermic, so there was always a certain amount of screaming, flapping of hands and running about clutching offspring to breasts when one made an appearance.

The poor misunderstood bees were really only interested in the arbour timbers, untreated wood which made an ideal nursery for their pupae. The sound of munching overhead as they excavated the nursery galleries with their jaws at the rate of an inch every six days was loud enough to be heard above conversation. A mixture of poo and sawdust sifted down on the heads of the inebriated or hatless, who would shortly be looking in the bathroom mirror wondering whether dandruff shampoos really worked. Every year the arbour got more rickety as bits of it crumbled and, finally, the bignonia, now more of a tree than a bush, was the only thing holding it up.

While Jack and Maud were away, another insect was at work: the dreaded sand fly, which is neither a fly nor anything to do with sand. Because of this silly, misleading name, thousands of dogs are infected every year, their owners unaware of the danger of Leishmaniasis spread by the tiny but deadly host. It's a disease of dogs in Europe, dismissed by doctors who think that humans cannot catch this leprosy look-alike that eats away at the extremities, despite the fact that 80 per cent of Brazilian troops on exercise in the South American jungles catch the disease. It's treatable (in humans) if caught early enough, but is generally fatal to dogs. By the time Jack and Maud returned three weeks later, Sabre was a very sick dog; thin, stary-coated, with an enlarged liver and his wet black nose dry and covered in crusty scabs. Jack's live-in English couple, knowing nothing of Leishmaniasis, had been hoping he would get better.

Jack had returned in a good mood and with a new car – complete with fourteen trout he had caught in Scotland stored in an icebox in the boot – but this disaster completely ruined their homecoming. The vet started Sabre on a treatment that would alleviate the symptoms, and the kennel windows were covered with netting to keep out the nocturnal insects, but the damage was done.

June was as flaming as it usually is on the Costa del Sol, but the weather was better than our prospects of making a living from guests. As we waved goodbye to the *pez gordo* (big cheese, literally big fish in Spanish) from Westland Helicopters and his charming wife, we were uncomfortably aware that the flow of tourists seemed to have dried up and we had no more bookings until the autumn. This came as a bit of a shock, particularly as we had managed to edge in front of Penny and Nigel in guest numbers for the first time during the spring, and were getting to like the sensation of knowing where our next meal was coming from.

In the short term it didn't matter – James had building work scheduled for months ahead and, having finished the apartments in Torremolinos, I was angling to do another apartment makeover; it was fun and paid well. I'd also started the brochure for Murray's ten houses, Joe's house was going ahead, the building industry all over the Costa del Sol was going at full blast – everything seemed set fair for more development and expansion. So why did we feel uneasy?

Our lack of bookings was part of the reason. There had been a gradual month-on-month improvement over the two years we'd been open for business, as 'word of mouth' had kicked in to bolster advertising in newspapers and magazines, on club notice boards and flyers. What had changed? We talked to Nigel and Penny, who reluctantly admitted that they had no bookings until September either. As we began to question others in the 'hospitality industry', we realised that the situation wasn't quite as rosy as the travel and construction industries would have us believe. There were vacancies in the holiday hotels and the bars and restaurants – normally bursting at the seams by July – welcomed us with open arms into their empty seats.

The English newspapers were full of articles about the booming property market and the strength of the UK economy, which was supported by my stepdaughter's husband, who appeared out of the blue to take us to dinner.

'Yeah, the business is going well, *really* well, we've just built a new showroom,' David told us, ordering a bottle of champagne. 'I'm never in England for more than a week or so at a time. Jill just stays at home and plays with her horses now – she can't stand all the travelling, even with the executive jet.'

'An *executive jet*?' I drooled jealously.

'It makes sense Alex...the company leases it. I get more work done, arrive bright-eyed and bushy-tailed, and don't have to worry about the baggage handlers being on strike. Everyone's happy.'

'David,' I said, 'there's something I've always wanted to know... When I was flying, even with the Cessna 172, you had to land if you had one coffee too many, or at least the girls did. On these small jets, what happens when you need to... you know, go?'

'Dead cunning bit of gear' he laughed. 'You lift up the cushion on one of the seats. The loo looks a bit like a flowerpot and its got male and female attachments.' His hands made explicit shapes.

'You mean you have to use this flowerpot with everyone watching?' I gasped in horror.

'Well...er... yes. I mean, it's at the far end, quite discreet, and you'd ask anyone else to turn away and chat among themselves. It wouldn't do to get distracted – everything gets sucked away into the jet stream – one moment of inattention and you could have the longest twizzle in history!' His face screwed up into an expression of agony and we all burst into heartless laughter.

Jill, my first husband's eldest daughter, had always been sensible, and I had to agree with her that the romance of executive jet flight had some painful drawbacks, despite its glamorous image.

At least my Quicksilver didn't have this problem, although some people would argue that flying micros is a good cure for constipation. On my last flight from the Moorland Microlight Flying Club (at Davidstow in Cornwall), I'd discovered the hard way that what goes up doesn't always come down very readily, whatever the theory of gravity maintains.

It was that rare thing, a perfect summer's day. A blazing sun had burned off the surface moisture from the heather and tiny, white, cotton-wool cloudlets only made the blue sky a more cerulean shade. Having done a few warm-up circuits, I was enjoying the flight, the freshness of the air, the crinkled blue of the sea fringing the pony-dotted moor – everything was perfect in my little aerial kingdom of the free and it was time to practice some 'touch and go' landings. I gently pushed the stick 'down'...then a bit harder... then really rather violently – with absolutely no result. The little canvas and aluminium tri-axis kept gaining height on the booming thermal from the wartime bomber runway below. Side-slipping and further frenzied stick pushing had no effect and I began to get rattled; this just doesn't happen in a conventional light aircraft, as you simply pour on more power and force your way down.

'How do I get this demented deckchair down?' I bellowed at a passing seagull, who gave me a sneery glance out of a cold, yellow eye as if to say: 'If God had meant you to fly...'

Even at 2,000 feet I could hear the howls and sobs of laughter from my husband and my instructor as they lay on their backs in the warm sun below, nursing beverages and enjoying the aerial struggle between woman and low technology. Woman won in the end, plopping the microlight down to ironic applause while hoping that an overlooked total eclipse of the sun would hide my embarrassment.

Despite the lighter than air incident, that day had been a high spot, but it was now obvious that bringing the Quickie to Spain had been a mistake. I was never going to have enough time to use it from the nearest club at Antequera – a good hour and a half away – or enough money to make a runway at the *finca*. Reluctantly I advertised it for sale or share. Several would-be flyers came to see it, including a man in a wheelchair. Most of them were bull-shitters who didn't even have a licence – the rest couldn't afford it – so I was delighted when an experienced commercial pilot phoned to say he was interested. Brian was recently retired, bored and missing his flying, so it looked like this could be just the thing for him. We dragged Quickie out of the barn where she had roosted for so long and assembled her in Brian's garden. James ran the engine up, everything seemed fine and the boys volunteered to take her to Seville for a trial flight.

❧

The hunters and their *galgos* (lurcher-like hunting dogs) were down in the arroyo again, in a replay of poor Luigi's death. The dogs had treed a cat – probably one of Antonio's – and were baying as they climbed into the branches. James got to them before the hunters, however, leaping down-slope through the olive trees, and with one well-aimed stone brought the lead dog tumbling out of the tree. He ordered the hunters off our land and, amazingly, they went (they had the right to traverse the land, there being no law of trespass).

The cat got away, thank goodness, but I didn't sleep well that night thinking about my poor Luigi and, during a wakeful period, I heard some odd noises outside. Throwing on some clothes and taking my target air-pistol, I went outside into the moonlight. Traudl was away and had asked us to keep an eye on her house, so I was perturbed to see two men with sacks in their hands creeping through her garden, shining rather dim torches over the walls of her villa. Waving the ancient pistol – which was guaranteed to do no damage unless inserted up a nostril – I couldn't come up with the Spanish equivalent of 'Reach for the sky,' so instead shouted quaveringly, 'who are you, what are you doing?' It didn't have the same ring, but the men stopped and shone their torches into my eyes instead.

Eyeing the pistol one of them falsettoed, '*No problema Señora*, no need for a gun, we are the snail catchers.'

Forgetting the hardware, I rubbed my head, nearly jamming the pistol up my sinus; this wasn't the reply I'd been expecting.

'Um, well, perhaps you'd like some of my snails?' I replied ingratiatingly.

'*Si si, muchas gracias Señora*, goodnight,' they grinned, falling on our garden like gourmet Vikings.

Snails were frequently on the menu at the Goat and Garlic, but I'd never thought deeply about where they came from; now I knew.

For Sunday lunch we occasionally went to a *venta* for a cheap meal, and one Sunday we ended up at a new place between Coín and Marbella. Throughout the meal cats wandered under the tables begging for food and one kitten in particular was making a bit of a nuisance of itself. One of the diners complained to the proprietor, who snatched up the kitten, walked across the main road and dumped it in the back of a gravel lorry in the car park. I couldn't believe what we were seeing and when the kitten emerged, teetered on the tailgate and dropped with a thud to the ground – obviously intending to run back across the road – it was too much. Finding a gap in the traffic, I ran across the road and picked up the scrawny little tortoiseshell.

'Don't you dare,' hissed James, 'we've got enough cats as it is.'

'But we can't just leave it to get run over, or for that bastard to put it in another lorry...'

'It's their cat, you can't just walk off with it.' James was losing the battle and knew it.

'Okay, I'll ask them for it.' The owner looked a bit startled and hesitated, probably wondering if he could extort money for the kitten.

'*Si, Señora*, take the *gatito*,' said the owner's wife quickly. And so we took Chica home.

12.
El Gato Macho

Stroppy in-yer-face teenagers are the same everywhere, in all species, and Muppet was a good example of why they get a bad press. He took an instant jealous dislike to Chica, stalking her to nip and paw-punch when he thought no one was looking; the only advantage was it took the pressure off Smoo, who had put up with his bullying and food grabbing with quiet dignity. But matters deteriorated when Muppet's pubescent testosterone kicked in and he started spraying; everywhere, everyone, everything, every twenty minutes. It was as if he remembered the Churchyard beetles and was trying to outdo them on an industrial scale – he succeeded beyond his wildest dreams.

This hideous episode happened over Christmas and I spent most of the holiday running around the house with a bowl of warm water and disinfectant, trying to remove the miasmic stench that clung to every vertical surface and most horizontal ones. Only when the crisis was resolved did Celia Haddon's column about pet problems in the *Daily Telegraph* inform me that this was the worst thing I could have done: disinfectant smells to cats like pee – a rival male cat's pee – so they have to mark *over* (and over) the place you've just washed. One of the guests nicknamed him Hung Too Hi – in a not entirely friendly manner – and it was obvious. *Something had to be done!*

As soon as the holiday was over, James grappled Muppet into the travelling cage – getting off lightly with only a few lacerations to his arm – and we took our problem cat to the vet.

'*Buenos días Señores*,' smiled the immaculate, white-coated vet as he took the cage and peered in. The smile faltered slightly as the whiff hit him and Muppet snarled, but he didn't miss a beat. 'Hmmm...he's a big cat...don't worry though. Just leave him with us, come back at five o'clock this afternoon and he'll be ready to go.'

When we returned at five the vet didn't seem quite so dapper. His Persil-white coat had some nasty stains and smelled dreadful, and his shoes looked as though they could do with a polish. He handed over the comatose Muppet with a look of reluctant respect. '*Su gato Muppet es muy, muy macho,*' he muttered to James in awed tones. 'He is the most *macho* cat I have ever cut.' He held out a hand strip-lynched with plasters and shook James's hand. 'Good luck, be sure to keep him in until he's fully conscious.'

We took him home and put the cage in a dark corner behind the gas cylinders. Later, the eerie howl of a vampire panther and a jiggling 58lb gas cylinder signalled that he was awake and trying to get out. Psychologically, he took a couple of days to get over his considerable loss, but it didn't interfere with his appetite.

It took us a bit longer; despite leaving the car doors and windows open, it was weeks before we could drive anywhere without the eau-de-tomcat drenched interior making us feel queasy.

The constant drizzle of hormones circulating around the *finca* had obviously affected Smoo as well, but I didn't worry too much when I went out on the terrace early one morning and found him mounting Chica with an expression of total concentration tinged with triumph. For a start, Chica was still a kitten, although a rapidly growing one who was putting on weight by the day. Secondly, Smoo had been given the chop years previously and I'd never seen this deviant behaviour before. I put the whole thing down to Muppet and his pernicious influence on every living thing in his vicinity.

∾

Traudl came for coffee one morning with some startling news: she was in love and engaged to be married. It was the first time I'd seen her really happy; laughter and animation transformed her face until it was almost pretty. Her normally dirty-blonde hair – which she washed infrequently with kitchen detergent – shone wheat-gold with health and salon pampering. She was wearing a casual but expensive-looking outfit and a diamond ring, and as she flashed it over the coffee mugs the story poured out.

'Everyzink iss changed, und I vill sell my *finca*,' she bubbled. 'Mine Eugene iss vairy clever und rich.'

Her fiancé was an academic but, unlike most of his species, he was independently wealthy. They planned to live in England, although they would keep his Fuengirola apartment, which would be his wedding present to her. They would have a pleasant academic life, with lots of travel and gracious living.

'I vill be giffing ze tea parties,' she giggled. 'Eugene says all ze ozzer professor's viffes give ze tea parties, so pliss tell me vat I must do.'

'Piece of cake Traudl. Just remember to heat the teapot first, cut the sandwiches thin and serve the most important wife first.'

'Zat is me, I vill be ze most important viff.'

I looked suitably impressed. 'Well, offer it to the second most important then...You'll be able to tell which one she is 'cos she'll look like she's chewing on a wasp. How did you meet Eugene?'

'At ze Lonely Hearts Club in Fuengirola. He ask me to dance. It vas *soo* romantica.'

I could feel my jaw sagging and managed to snap it shut. 'That's wundabar, I mean wonderful Traudl – my husband and I wish you both all the best for the future.'

And we did: Traudl wasn't the sharpest knife in the box and she'd had a miserable first marriage, so she deserved some good fortune and had gone out and grabbed it.

Unfortunately I also felt wildly, green-eyed jealous, and a glance in the mirror would have shown someone sucking on a whole hornet's nest rather than one miserable wasp. Although I loved Tara and my husband, the thought of a cosy academic life in England sounded rather wonderful. And a couple of new dresses that hadn't come from a *segundo mano* stall in Fuengirola flea market wouldn't go amiss either.

Out of the blue, I was also struck by a *coup de foudre*: I needed to write the children's book bobbing around in my head and didn't have time for longhand or my pebble-dashed-with-

Tippex typing. Mikey, the son of a doctor friend from San Pedro, had started a business selling computers and software so he was the obvious person to ask. He agreed to bring a machine to the *finca* and give me a lesson. It all sounded delightfully simple and pastoral: rams, mice and flops – surely it must be easy-peasy to someone who enjoyed gadgets and I looked forward to getting to grips with the latest technology.

The lesson was a disaster: nothing made the slightest sense and it didn't help that Mikey only spoke when it was totally unavoidable and used the barest minimum of words. This wasn't bloody-mindedness, simply that from early childhood he had preferred not to speak. As the baby in a highly vocal family, he probably just couldn't be bothered to keep interrupting, and it became a restful habit. Despite being orally challenged, Mikey was of above average intelligence and managed to lead a full business and social life. As a teacher, however, he left a few corners unswept. By the time Mikey roared off in his Alfa – fingering his throat like a singer at the conclusion of the Ring Cycle – I was nearer to tears than to being able to use my new purchase. The next day was no better: documents refused to save and disappeared into the ether; commands and warnings flashed and bleeped; and the only bytes were from my very user-unfriendly machine. Cursing men and their love of 'look at me' programming, manuals written in Spanish gibberese and all things pc, helped my temper, but didn't get me any closer to mastering Wordstar.

I'd been hoping to use the computer to help design Murray's brochures, but even designing a blank page seemed beyond me.

After 12 solid hours at the computer an odd message flashed up on the screen: HELP DESPAIR. The screen then went blank and the program crashed. It sounded like a cry from the machine itself but, being a Spanish-speaking pc, it should have been something like 'DESESPERACIÓN DE LA AYUDA'. That really would have been a worry, but, in the circumstances, I concluded that I'd had a small brainstorm and typed it myself, and that perhaps I should get out more.

Penny and Nigel had a computer, so I bumped down to La Questa in search of enlightenment, or at least an explanation of the most basic procedures. We hadn't been down there for a few weeks, so the changes in the place were startling. The garden looked tired and seared, and rubbish floated on the pool. The tennis court was cracked and the net lay on the ground in festoons. Something was very wrong.

Penny's explanation shocked me.

'We're giving up... We have to honour the arrangements already made of course, as some people have bought 'weeks' in the hovelettes, a bit like timeshare,' she explained. 'We sold off weeks to raise capital and we won't be able to pay those people back unless we can sell the place. It'll be put on the market and we won't be looking for more bookings.'

Penny looked thinner and her usual energy and bounce was muted. 'Nigel has got a job down on the coast selling property,' she continued, 'and I'm looking for a job as well...'

That evening James and I sat under the Carpenter-bee bower with a glass of wine and talked about this development. It was sad and worrying – they had never been rivals in any unpleasant sense and, in fact, had sent us business. We needed to take a long hard look at what we were doing, and decide whether the downturn in tourism on the Costa meant that we too should look more actively for alternative sources of income.

The brochure for Murray's ten houses was finally finished and looked pleasingly professional. James helped with the illustrations (he was brilliant at technical drawing) and we managed to make the meanly-specified bungalows as attractive as possible, with lashings of trees and flowers around the pool and traditional ochre detailing on the windows. Murray seemed delighted and I gave him my invoice.

'Fine, Alex... leave it with me. I'll get these off to the printer,' he said. 'The villas will sell like hot cakes, no problem.'

I didn't insist that Murray settle up right away, although I needed the money to pay for the computer. I knew he had cash-flow problems and, after all, he was a friend.

That night I had a vivid dream – more of a nightmare really – about an earthquake violently shaking the house. The aftermath – digging down and excavating the foundations to see whether they were strong enough – seemed really important, but the relief of finding that they were solid was palpable. I awoke up feeling relieved, then immediately felt terrified again because the dream had seemed more a warning about the real world than the usual rag-bag of the unconscious. When I was cleaning the pool mid-morning a neighbour from across the valley stopped for a chat.

'Come in and have a coffee Eileen,' I said. 'I'm ready for a break. Had a lousy night... how's Bill?'

'Ee, ya knaw, reet grand Bill,' replied Eileen in her broad Yorkshire accent, 'Out'n shed, werkin as usual, we 'ardly meet these days. I've been 't Grande to see a patient, silly sod's got to 'ave a foot chopped off, diabetes ya knaw, an he war'nt taking t'pills.'

I liked Eileen. She didn't mince her words, but the crusty exterior hid a kind heart.

'Ave ya heerd about t'earthquake?'

My heart lurched uncomfortably. 'What earthquake Eileen – where, when, here?' I babbled. 'I dreamt about an earthquake last night. That's why I didn't sleep too well...' sweat popped out and trickled down my neck.

' Oh ay? Cud be 'ere and all, quake 'it Malaga before times – they reckon it fer next week.' Eileen heaved herself out of the chair. 'Gotta get back an fettle Bill.'

She got into her 4x4 and trundled off down the track as I put the biscuits away and washed the cups.

'Eh, ehhmm, Alex...' Eileen stood in the doorway, shaking her head. 'Me waggen's int' ditch, is James around t'give me an 'and?'

'What happened Eileen? Are you okay?' There was a deep ditch on one side, but Eileen was used to our rough track.

'It were a bit strange Alex... I looked in t'rear mirrer, 'an there were a reet evil liddle black face peepin over m'shoulder. Give me sich a frit I drove int' ditch. Bill'l kill me if she's dented.'

'Ohhh, no... no, that bloody Muppet!' I moaned. I knew exactly what had happened: he loved travelling in cars and would get into any vehicle left open. It wasn't the first time he'd popped up from a back seat to frighten someone.

It wasn't too difficult getting her wagon out of the ditch and as soon as Eileen had left I went down to Malaga to try to get earthquake insurance for the house. My dream and what Eileen had said seemed too much of a coincidence and I was petrified.

It was a waste of time because none of the companies seemed keen to offer earthquake insurance and I returned home depressed and convinced Finca Tara would soon be sliding down the hill into the *arroyo*. Strangely, there was an earthquake in the Mediterranean the next day – but only a mild one – in Greece. The biggy was a week later in Western Iran, where 40-50,000 people died, 60,000 were injured and 400,000 made homeless. I felt like we'd had a lucky escape.

The earthquake scare threw a different light on Finca Tara, its underpinnings and the surrounding countryside. The reluctant conclusion was that we were perched on a sand dune and the biblical injunction to 'Build not thy house upon sand' – even a multi-million-year-old sand dune – still holds good in an earthquake, when sand becomes liquid and flows like water. From the mountain kraut's eyrie you could see our valley and it was easy to imagine what it might have looked like in the Cretaceous: a wrinkle in the gigantic, estuarine vista of what would be the Guadalhorce river delta 144 million years later. It would have been interesting to see through the eyes of the dinosaur that had left a scarily-large vertebral bone in our garden, unearthed by the oxen ploughing.

෴

It was now all too obvious that the hanky panky I'd seen between Smoo and Chica wasn't as innocent as previously imagined. Sixty days later Chica was still growing, but a certain part of her anatomy was growing faster than the other bits. My poor little kitten was about to become a poor little mother.

She chose to have her kittens in the courtyard, under the impenetrable umbrella of a fern in a Chinese fish bowl. The calico kitten was promised to some English friends nearby, but the tabby image of his dad we kept, naming him Merlin. Shortly after his eyes opened and he started exploring his surroundings, Merlin vanished into thin air. Standing in the courtyard next to the fishbowl nest we could hear the faintest elfin echo of a meow, which kept us searching, but it was only after several hours of going over every inch of the surrounding house and garden that we realised it was coming from the earth beneath our feet. He had crawled through a tiny hole in a broken airbrick into the *pozo negro* and was crouched on a ledge, inches from a literally s****y death. James broke open the *pozo,* allowing him to crawl free, and we renamed him Houdini in the hope that it would help him escape any further mischief of this kind.

෴

My mother, Hope, didn't care for flying much, but she wanted to come and warm her bones, and someone made the brilliant suggestion that she travel by train. Mum was notoriously scatty, blind as a bat and up for anything, so we were slightly concerned that she might get shunted into a siding in Zagreb for a fortnight with a bunch of itinerant, card-sharp, Albanian coke-heads. Luckily, her friend and next-door-neighbour Deirdre liked the idea too, so she was designated as Keeper-of-the-Specs and Tickets. The ladies set out for Andalucia with smart straw hats and lots of books, arriving at Malaga station with elongated arms, the result of heaving luggage during a totally porter-free journey, but otherwise in good health and spirits.

James took them to Malaga for a shopping trip. There had been a bout of 'ride by' robberies by youths on scooters or bikes going on in the city, so James walked behind them as a guard. Unfortunately, he stopped to look in a shop window just as Hope and Deirdre speeded up, and he looked up to see two youths on a motorbike in the act of snatching my mother's bag. She hung on grimly, with Deirdre screaming at her to let it go, and James accelerating rapidly towards them, but it was too professional. The youth kicked my mother's shin, whipped out a knife and cut the strap of her bag. James was so close that he nearly caught hold of the toe-rag's shirt as he swung up behind his mate, but his arm was an inch too short and they accelerated away into the traffic.

A Spanish man walking his Alsatian reacted quickly, releasing his dog to streak after the thieves and calling the police. The dog didn't catch them either, but the police put up roadblocks and *did* catch them.

James was subpoenaed as a witness when the case came up and we were sent to the fourth floor of the impressive Law Courts, where we joined a crowd of shifty-eyed desperadoes lounging uneasily against the marble walls. They turned out to be witnesses and we soon acquired the same look when we discovered there were no drinks – not even a water fountain – and no loos. It made sense, in a way, because if you don't drink you won't need a lavatory, and if you can't go to the lavatory you won't miss your call. There was no way of telling what time your case would come to court as they didn't work down or even across a list, but slalomed through it in a random manner.

Every now and then counsel would appear and give some tone to the proceedings. I couldn't take my eyes off one with shoulder-length blond hair, a white silk shirt and black silk ski pants, set off with silver and gold shoes, the whole ensemble topped off by a Regency-style coat with a deeply-shawled collar, nipped waist and full gathered skirt. As the women were wearing much the same outfit – with the addition of a silver or gold handbag – it seemed this must be formal wear to aid recognition of the law.

After a couple of hours, a handcuffed youth manacled to a policeman and surrounded by three other burly policemen entered the room.

'That's HIM,' James hissed. He had been a bit worried about whether he would recognise the mugger again. We all hung around for another hour, while I itched to kick his shins, then they all whirled away – prisoner, counsel and police – and we were told that the case was postponed until tomorrow because the second judge hadn't turned up.

The next day was a reprise of the first except that we brought a bottle of water with us and the mugger was handcuffed to the biker. The case was on. James asked for an interpreter and was underwhelmed when a ragged, unshaven, dangerous-looking man with one shoe and a dictionary appeared. It soon became apparent that James's Spanish was slightly better than the ragged guy's English – even with a dictionary – and he was able to dispense with the 'interpreter', managing perfectly well on his own. This went down well with the judge, who thanked James profusely for his penal awareness and sent the two perps down for four and a half years.

This was some slight consolation to my mother, who had her handbag back: a bag containing a comb, handkerchief, spectacle case and around two pounds in cash. The kick had bruised her leg so badly that it ulcerated for months. As the sentences for this sort of crime became harsher, *moto* bag-snatching (almost miraculously) went out of fashion in Malaga.

৵

Penny had also found a job on the coast and to celebrate, she and Nigel threw a party. The whole gang of us trooped off to La Questa and almost fell out of our cars with shock. The place was immaculate. Nigel and Penney's hovelette – bare cement walled for the four years they had been there, apart from the eastern skyline mural that James had painted for their Ali Babathemed New Year's Eve party – now sported pristine whitewash and new curtains; woodwork sparkled and windows gleamed. The garden paths meandered trimly again and the eastern-style food was delicious.

'Bit of a difference since I last saw it,' Jack said. 'You seem to have cleaned the place up at last!'

'Shush Jack,' muttered Maud.

'Well it's true, bloody awful mess it was ... Mmm, these rolls are good. Do you have any chutney?'

The door opened and a diminutive brown-skinned couple in white jackets came in, bringing yet more food.

'I'd like you all to meet our Filipino housekeepers,' Nigel said into the surprised silence.

'Harroo,' they chorused, giving us all beaming smiles.

'Bloody hell,' muttered Jack into his Rioja as he looked at the array of delicious dishes on the snowy cloths, framed with glittering silver and crystal. 'Wish I could find a couple like this.'

13.
Goodbye to the Captain

The weekly phone call to my parents had been worrying: my father was in hospital for tests, but it was nothing serious according to my mother. She hadn't, however, sounded quite as convinced about the triviality of his symptoms as I would have liked and I ran a computer biorhythm programme to check his condition. What it indicated made me drive to Fuengirola and book a ticket on the next plane – I knew my father was in great danger. On his last visit to Spain some months before his lack of appetite had been a sign that something wasn't right. In a photo of him cuddling kitten Muppet he looked thin and drawn, but his doctor didn't think there was anything to worry about. Now there obviously was.

Arriving at my parents' farmhouse in the depths of the Dorset countryside I found a note from my mother on the kitchen table to say that she was at the hospital, so I got back in the hire car and drove to Dorchester. My father was awkwardly propped against a ramp of pillows, his cornflower-blue eyes and striped pyjamas a shocking contrast to his waxy pale skin. Even his thick hair was whiter than when I'd last seen him.

'How are you Pa?'

'I'm fine... don't like this hospital though, the nurses are all bloody ugly.'

My mother looked exhausted. 'If you're going to stay Alex, I'll go home and feed the animals.'

'Yeah, you go on home Mum. See you when I see you.'

I turned back to my Pa, to see his eyes full of love and gratitude.

'Thanks for coming – I'd been hoping you would.'

'Are you in pain?'

He shook his head. 'No, not any more.' He lifted his wrist with the attached morphine pump. 'I'm perfectly all right. Don't know what all the fuss is about.'

I kissed him and sat beside his bed while the bravest man I've ever known set sail for the last time – 20 minutes later he was gone.

Shockingly, after a lifetime of disliking my father – even fearing him – it was only in the moment of his death that I knew I loved him.

After ringing my mother, I went to Maiden Castle – a huge iron-age hill fort that towers over Dorchester – and walked for a while, my father still with me as his life drifted through my mind. The young subaltern going out to India with his regiment; the posting to Egypt; the fall on the polo field that led him to contract polio and be invalided out of the Army; and the battle with anger and depression that followed. My mother enters the story now as she swam in Brixham harbour; finding herself exhausted, she hauled herself onto the deck of a yacht and met a handsome young yachtsman with a limp and a useless, withered right arm. A wedding followed quickly and the decision to sail around the world in a converted Swedish lifeboat. (But that's another story.)

My father spent the war in a desk job, involved – but not nearly as much as he would have liked – in the defence of his country. And after the war? A succession of dairy farms where my parents struggled to keep their heads above water with a conspicuous lack of success. This was hardly surprising because my father had no aptitude for farming whatsoever, and couldn't even drive a nail into a wall without bringing the wall down. My poor father had a hard, disappointing life after a golden youth that promised everything; he'd been a superb athlete, excelling at cricket, riding and rowing. He even played tennis against Fred Perry at Wimbledon. A career in the Army was all he ever wanted and it was his, until a dirty Egyptian hospital ward ended it all with a spell in an Iron Lung. No wonder he had a violent temper.

14.
The Last White Queen
of Sarawak

After the initial relief and pleasure at having me there, my mother's attitude changed to a subtle hostility. It seemed that, in some covert way, it was my fault that she was now a widow and my attempts to persuade her to move from the large, remote farmhouse to something smaller and more manageable were seen as high-handed interference. It was time to go before we started a row that would be difficult to stop.

The sadness and tensions of my Pa's death probably triggered the crippling back problem that struck the day before I was due to fly back to Spain. It was bad, but with a handful of painkillers it was possible to walk with the help of a stick, so it seemed best not to change the arrangements, particularly as we had guests booked. James could knock up a perfectly competent 'heart attack on a plate', but he couldn't be expected to chef a *table d'hôte* every evening. I boarded the London train with too much luggage, a white stick ma had used when she had cataracts and a .410 shotgun of my father's that I'd always liked.

Victoria Station didn't have any porters – at least not at the entrance the taxi driver dumped me at, before accelerating away with my unread newspaper still on the seat. Gratefully I grabbed a luggage trolley and heaved my cases onto it – causing a wave of nausea as pain lanced through my back and leg – only to discover why it had been abandoned. Half pushing and half leaning on the wonky-wheeled trolley, I tacked across the concourse like a sinking dinghy in a stiff nor-easterly, following the signs for the 'advance baggage check' until a notice barred the way at the bottom of an escalator. 'NO TROLLEYS' it said. I stood and looked at the notice for a long time. The people getting on the escalator all seemed to be mums with babies, or elderly people with neat little wheeled suitcases, so no help there.

'Excuse me, could you tell me if there's a lift to the baggage check anywhere?' I asked a ticket inspector.

The British Rail Amazon, whose uniform was losing the brave struggle to contain her magnificent breasts and rear *embonpoint,* swung around and stared down at me – the lowest form of life, a clueless passenger.

'Take the escalatah.' She waved a ham-sized hand in the general direction of St. John's Wood and returned to humiliating a flustered housewife with the wrong sort of day ticket.

'But...*please*, I can't get my luggage up the escalator, I've hurt my back,' I whined in my best supplicant tone.

Her pupils were blacker than her ebony skin, but the whites of her eyes were a curious, almost glowing cherry red. There was no question that she had both the physical and psychological advantage in this battle of wills. My eyes dropped.

'Hmmn... Ain't no lift for passengeahs, but maybe there's a goods lift ovah behind theah.'

A vigorous search revealed a McDonald's Hamburger Heaven, a stall selling porno mags and a punk being unwell, although it was difficult to say whether it was beavers or BSE troubling him.

There was no sign of a lift, of course. I tacked back to the Amazon.

She nodded slightly, acknowledging a tiresome reappearance. '*Benjamin!*' she suddenly hollered, still looking straight at me.

The fright sent another jolt searing through my back and it must have showed because her expression softened fractionally. She turned to the only working porter in Victoria Station, who'd materialised beside me. 'Benjamin, my main man, you knows this heah station. You mind a lift to baggage check?'

Benjamin pursed his lips in thought and finally nodded. 'Yass, I mind there's a lift roun the back o' ticket two.'

The ticket inspector glanced at the gun case lying on top of the cases. 'Tak this...lady... to theah lift Benjamin.'

Benjamin not only took me to the lift, he also pushed the trolley to the baggage check and got me on the Gatwick train, for which the lady was duly grateful.

Gatwick was easier because I'd phoned ahead to book a wheelchair, which came with a personal carer called Les who would remain with me until I boarded the plane. Les was a saint – from the moment I collapsed, almost sobbing with relief, into the wheelchair, to his management of the licences and permits needed to take a gun and ammunition on board a plane – the service was faultless.

I felt like the last white Queen of Sarawak being pushed by my bearer, shotgun and white stick clutched between my knees, as we hurtled back and forth across the airport looking for various officials and elastic to bind the cartridges together in the manufacturer's box, a mystifying but apparently vital procedure. The only assistance that Les offered which was happily turned down was the 'toileting aid', although I'm sure he would have been as deft and discreet as any nurse. Les's outrageous gossip about the VIPs passing through the airport had me in fits of laughter, as did his spats with his bullishly-macho and insensitive supervisor. 'He's an absolute *callous swine* Mrs Browning,' he confided tearfully and, although sympathetic, I had to pinch myself to stop laughing out loud.

During our frequent to-ings and fro-ings past the 'disabled care' desk, a little drama unfolded as a well-refreshed family demanded a wheelchair for their Dai, who wasn't feeling too well.

'Have you booked a wheelchair Madam?' asked the desk clerk.

'No *bach,* but our Dai needs a wheelchair, his legs aren't too good see?'

'May I ask, what condition is he suffering from Madam?'

'No, there's nothing *wrong* with him *cariad*, he's had a lovely farewell party, an his legs aren't too good now.'

'Well, I'm sorry Madam, but we don't provide a wheelchair service for *that* sort of disability.' The clerk managed to combine a caring tone with a sneer in the direction of the green-tinged Dai, who was slumped at a table surrounded by his music-loving family.

His lady wife's face clouded over. 'Disgusting I call it, we pay our taxes for this sort of thing and then you can't get no help when you need it... We'll be making a complaint to our MP, you see if we don't!' She lurched away, leaning into an invisible gale.

At the boarding desk, there was a tired-looking, elderly, Arab gentleman asking about a stand-by ticket. As Les muttered to the staff and handed over my papers, I made an anodyne remark about hoping they'd find him a seat. Then came the call to board the plane and Les wheeled me past a long queue, which included the tired and emotional Dai, who gave me a poisonous look.

'*Some* people manage to wangle a free ride, isn't it?' he remarked in stentorian tones.

The queue looked at me with interest.

'*Some* people know how to play the system, like Lady Muck here.'

The interest turned to disgust and a few people giggled.

A pubescent blush scalded me from scalp to waist as Les tutted and pushed the chair down the ramp – into the totally unexpected comfort of First Class.

'*Oooh*, people can be so *catty* Mrs B, you deserve a little spoiling.' Les manoeuvred my damply-rigid body into the seat and squeezed my hand, managing an innocently startled expression on finding a crisp banknote adhering to his palm.

A few minutes later, the elderly Arab gentleman I'd seen at the gate dropped into the seat next to me. We chatted and soon photos of his 18 grandchildren were produced and admired. He told me that Bahrainis were the poor men of the Arab world and I sympathised with him over having to make do with a miserably cramped, four-bedroom apartment opposite the Dorchester. When the duty-free trolley arrived he purchased a few things and handed me a large bottle of Rochas' Byzance perfume. 'It was so nice of you to worry about me,' he said with a sweet smile.

I started the usual British 'No, I couldn't possibly accept...' routine, then stopped, and relaxed. It was a nice gesture, not an invitation to join his harem, and I accepted graciously; in my book, perfume wins over a bag of candied sheep's eyes any day.

My benefactor asked if he could drop me off anywhere in his limo, but I knew James would be there to meet me, so we said our farewells as the plane bumped to a stop on the Malaga tarmac.

The wheelchair brigade – consisting of myself and another woman – were manhandled off the plane and into a plain van containing two mediaeval contrivances latched to the floor with car door handles to hold the chairs in place. The attendants locked our chairs down, ignoring Dai, who had mysteriously appeared again, intent on making a last minute bid for medical aid. The attendants shrugged and explained in machine-gun Spanish that there wasn't any room for him, but Dai wasn't going to be denied a second time; he'd obviously had a few more drinks on board and was now terminally tired and emotional. Finally, they gave in and pointed to the attendant's bench at the far end of the van. The chair-lift rose with the swaying Dai on it and he gave me a look of triumph as he surged across the van with his clinking carrier bag. His foot snagged on one of the door handles in the floor and he lurched across the vehicle, ending up perched on the other lady's lap.

'*Dai bach,* you sheep-shagging asshole, sit down and shut up!' I said loudly and firmly in my best Ceredigion-flavoured Welsh. Dai sat down very hard indeed and stared at me as if I'd turned into a black mamba. There wasn't another peep out of him, which was just as well because I'd exhausted my Welsh vocabulary learned after lights-out in boarding school. (Thank you Dawn Davies.)

I could see James behind the glass screen of the Baggage Hall and waved frantically for him to come and help with the luggage and customs. But he wasn't looking for a disabled person in a wheelchair and gazed over my head, searching for the fit, active woman he'd seen off a fortnight earlier. The crowd enjoyed the joke as I waved my stick and the attendant jumped up and down shouting '*Aqui*, Jaime, *aqui!*'

I tapped on the glass and James looked down with horrified recognition – I remembered that I hadn't had time to tell him about the slipped disc before I left Dorset.

It was the usual emotional reunion.

'What the blazes are you doing in that?'

'Back's gone again,' I said.

'Bad?'

'Yeah.'

'Shit.'

It was nice to be home again, in funny sinky Tara.

❧

How exciting to find the very rare *Lineman Ibericus Telefonicus* erecting a telegraph pole in our garden – we started thinking that maybe, just maybe, we were going to get a telephone line. The young lad slid down the pole rather too rapidly, bringing tears to his eyes, to put us right.

'*No, Señores, lo siento,* I'm sorry, we're just putting the poles up, it will be at least another year before the exchange is enlarged.' He pointed at the pole. 'Maybe you would like to go up?' He offered his linesman's belt and flapped a hand at a bee circling his head.

James and I reluctantly turned down this tempting offer and evaded bees of our own. Hanging from a branch was what looked like a dark, furry supermarket bag. A deep, low hum came from the solid, yet liquidly restless mass – a bee swarm. A yelp was heard from the pole next to Traudl's house, followed by another, and soon the five linesmen were running around the garden shouting and swatting madly at themselves. We retired to the kitchen and had a beer, while I smeared the linesmen's stings with a paste of baking powder. Thankfully when we went out again they seemed to have calmed down.

Wasps, bees and insects were a constant problem. It's difficult not to swat at them and I was always terrified that a child would get stung and have a bad reaction, but we were lucky. Praying mantises, however, were one of my favourites garden insects – their beautiful green and gold bodies and the strange intelligence in their triangular eyes attracted us; their insatiable appetite for aphids was a bonus. We put their papery-brown egg masses – like origami walnuts – under the rose bushes in the hope that the hundreds of microscopic, transparent nymphs would colonise the roses.

~

El Enano – Murray's development at Hacyenda Lopez – was finished, but hints to Murray that payment would be appreciated for the work I'd done on the brochures were ignored, so finally I asked for the money straight out. He grinned ruefully and pointed at a pile of papers on the table. 'Sorry Alex, no can do at this moment. I've got a stack of bills and nothing coming in.'

Short of suing him, which wasn't an option, that seemed to be that. I drove away feeling spineless for not having pursued payment right away and guilty about spending a lot of our money on a computer that wasn't paying for itself.

The local newspaper, *Sur in English*, carried expat advertising, and for the next few weeks we combed the ads looking for anything that would give a return on my impulsive buy. At last, there was something that seemed right up my street: an author in search of an editor for a technical book on tropical farming. Having sent a letter and CV, I phoned the advertiser expecting an enthusiastic response, only to be told that yes, I was a contender, but in a lineout of 52 other eager, experienced applicants. Furthermore, he had already chosen a lady who ticked every box. This was a bit of a blow: mentally I already had the job and had banked the money. Calling on every shred of Irish DNA in my body, I badgered Willem (the author) into giving me an interview as a 'back-up editor', in case things didn't work out with his first choice.

There wasn't much in the wardrobe that looked suitable for an on-the-ball businesswoman, but after brushing the green mould and cat hairs off my one respectable skirt and finding a mildewed leather briefcase, I sort-of looked the part. Luckily, the interview went well; I was promoted on the spot to second-in-line and Willem gave me a copy of the manuscript on disk to study. The job nearly ended right there and then, when in a flurry of self-congratulation and carelessness, I left the briefcase containing the precious disk and notes in a supermarket after doing a spot of shopping on the way home.

Ten days later Willem phoned to say that the Chosen One was useless because she didn't know her haploid from her diploid. I didn't either, but chutzpah paid off and, being a farmer's daughter, I'd got a bit of a head start when it came to editing a tome entitled *Raising & Sustaining Productivity of Smallholder Farming Systems in the Tropics: A Handbook of Sustainable Agricultural Development*.

It was exciting to get the work but, of course, there were a couple of flies in the soup: Willem had a very tight deadline of two months, which was extremely demanding for a highly technical book that weighed in at over 800 pages. To make matters worse, I still didn't fully understand the WordStar programme I'd be using – and we would be having guests during those two months. The bright spot was that one couple were old friends who could look after themselves, and Chris was a computer freak who used WordStar the whole time and knew it inside out. I constantly interrupted their naps beside the pool, dashing out to ask Chris some daft question, but he was very patient and my school friend Guinevere was uncomplaining and supportive when her husband was highjacked.

Working 14 hours a day the job got done in the allotted time. Willem came to stay for the last three days, before returning to Indonesia, just to make sure that everything was tied up. On the last morning he handed over the payment – the computer had earned its purchase price at last.

It felt like freedom after a spell in prison – I hadn't seen a lot of the sun for two months and a ride in the country on the Montesa seemed like a good idea. Half an hour and many miles away, I felt a tap on my right eyeball, almost as if an insect had hit my eye, but that wasn't possible because I was wearing goggles. By the time I got home, flashing lights and floating black spots jerking across my field of vision told me that something was amiss: next morning the affected eye had little vision at all and was also painful. There was definitely something wrong.

In *The Unbearable Lightness of Being,* Milan Kundera describes something rather similar, which turns out to be a detached retina. I knew that if it was that, it had to be dealt with quickly. It meant another trip to Gibraltar, this time to see an eye specialist at St Bernard's Hospital. Anyone who has had eye problems will know about the drops that open up the iris so that the back of the eye can be examined – they aren't very pleasant! But he had good news: at least it wasn't a detached retina. Resting his elbow on the top of a loo roll, his 'most valuable technical aid', he assured us that it was just a retinal tear or hole – there had been a haemorrhage, which had sealed itself, and the floaters were specks of blood which would gradually be reabsorbed. He couldn't say what had caused it or whether it would happen again, but it was possible that the unrelenting use of the computer could have had something to do with it. Leaving the institutional brown walls and torn lino, we emerged into blinding sunlight and I went into the cathedral to say a prayer of thanks that it wasn't literally blinding.

Joan raised the subject of Hacyenda Lopez over a coffee and a biscuit. 'Have you heard anything about what's going on up at the Hacyenda, Alex?'

'No, not a thing,' I replied, a bit curtly. Murray and Pixie weren't my favourite people at the time and I hadn't been near the place since the failed attempt to dun Murray into paying the bill.

'Well, I hear from Georg that they've set up a casino and high-rollers from the coast have been coming up here. I wouldn't be surprised – there seems to have been a lot of traffic around here at night recently.'

'Gosh, that sounds a bit dodgy. They can't have a licence, surely?'

We looked at each other and a naughty thought occurred to both of us.

'Shall we?' Joan murmured, 'Murray and Pixie are away at the moment, but David, Terry and Ruth are there...'

'Yes!'

We walked up the road to Hacyenda Lopez, gossiping about Murray's latest lot of tenants. Everyone had been friendly and had asked them to parties when they'd arrived, but some strange facts were emerging and people had begun to have second thoughts. The tenants were attracting a certain type of English expat: Georg, who was still living there, complained that there was always a crowd of drunk or drugged young men by the pool, running around naked with their equally sartorially-challenged bimbos. Georg was not in the least prudish, but he was bored with having to clean up after them and finally told them to b***** off, whereupon one of them pulled a knife and threatened him.

David, the most engaging of the three tenants, had enjoyed the sympathy vote to begin with. He had only one leg and his mother and her lover had run off with the money he'd left them to oversee the building of his house. The lustre wore off when the Lopez caretaker discovered that David had a GBH conviction in Britain for knifing a man. Let off with a caution, he went out the same day and knifed somebody else, then wisely legged it – or rather one-legged it – back to Spain. David's other weakness was that he wasn't keen on paying his bills: Juan had managed to get his bar bill settled by suggestively rolling a couple of cartridges under David's nose, but James, for some inexplicable reason, didn't seem too keen on collecting for the pool plumbing he'd installed at David's house.

The second tenant, Terry, was simply thick, and had just written off a borrowed Merc under the influence. As he put it rather aggrievedly, 'I 'adn't no idea these c****s drove on the wrong side of the f*****g road, did I?'

Ruth was a cheerful, still-pretty coke-head who enthusiastically copulated with anyone who could be persuaded to contribute to her fund for recreational substances.

Joan and I walked through the garden to the pool, where the three tenants were working on their all-over tans. They were happy to talk about the casino, which they enjoyed in the company of several other local English lads and, yes, they had seen several faces from Marbella. Terry good-naturedly took us to see it and we looked around in amazement. One of the apartments had been converted into one cavernous room, fitted out to the highest standard. Big padded chairs ringed the professional baize tables – set up for poker, blackjack and roulette – bathed in light from suspended lamps. Joan and I gawped, shell-shocked at the authentic atmosphere.

'Ruth's got a bit o'competition on party nights,' Terry grinned. 'Murray's got a couple of them bunny girls, they comes up 'ere in their costumes, phwhoaar! They don't 'arf sell some booze when they wiggles their cute little arses.'

Joan and I glanced at each other. We certainly knew what was going down now.

Not long after, Murray and Pixie returned from England and the 'casino' opened again. A month or two later everyone for miles around was awakened one night by the wail of police-car sirens sweeping through La Cabra towards Hacyenda Lopez. This was followed by the thunder and thrash of choppers circling overhead, their searchlights shredding the darkness.

Murray and Pixie must have had their escape route planned, as they left the back way by driving across the golf course as the law came in the front. They fled to England and the word was that Charlie Wilson (a notorious British criminal living on the Costa) and a few others were eager to have a friendly chat about money owing for fixtures and fittings, to say nothing of bunnies. Who knows whether a meeting took place or whether Murray simply had an unfortunate accident, but we heard on the grapevine that he was in hospital for a while with a leg injury.

A couple of the locals in Juan's Bar seemed to be on friendly terms with the local cops, who routinely dropped in for refreshment. Murray had sold these same locals a couple of the El Enano houses, trying to part them from their money without handing over the deeds. Part of the charm of the Spanish is their acceptance and trust of foreigners, but even they have their limits. Murray had made a gross mistake and done us all a great disservice if he thought they were stupid peasants – and that there would be no comeback.

15.
Up, Up and Away

With Willem and his book out of the way, we planned to get the microlight back in the air. Brian located a flying club near Seville that had a similar model and an instructor willing to test-pilot the Quicksilver. I had a full private pilots licence (PPL), but after four years with only a minimum of flights I wasn't confident enough to take her up on her maiden Spanish flight myself. Although Brian was happy to fly a 747 weighing 127 tons, he also had reservations as he'd never flown anything so small and flimsy. We both wondered whether the engine would be okay. James had fired it up on several occasions, but it's better to discover that you have a seriously unwell mill on the ground, rather than at two thousand feet. Brian and I both preferred to be live cowards rather than dead aviators. Or, as Rick, who had more hours in his logbook than Brian and I combined, put it: 'There are old pilots and there are bold pilots – but there are very few old bold pilots.' Rick started his commercial flying career in the '20s, when a flight to Cape Town meant weeks rather than hours – the first flight to Cape Town in 1920 – by Ryneveld and Brand in a Vickers Vimy – took six weeks!

Myself, James, Brian and his son Tim, trailed Quickie up to Seville and assembled her. Amazingly, nothing was broken or lost. James coaxed the engine into convincing life, the Spanish El Biggles, after the most cursory inspection, strapped on his goggles and bumped down the rough track they called a runway. He buzzed and banked and side-slipped above us in the last of the setting sun, then swooped back to earth as lightly as a bat in the gathering dusk, giving us a cheerful thumbs up as he trundled to a halt in front of his audience. Brian took some instruction during the day – although he had a current commercial licence, the difference between a jumbo and a microlight was so extreme that he needed tuition. However, after a couple of hours he was competent to pilot the Flying Lawnmower and to give me a refresher course.

James and I spent the night in the old quarter of Seville in a

little pension recommended by Penny. It was a pretty place –
with flowered balconies and a tiled internal courtyard – and
enticingly cheap, so we didn't grumble too much when the
wardrobe door fell off. Having hung my clothes on the now very
accessible rail, I went into the en suite to have a wash. There
wasn't time for a bath, so I used the bidet to refresh myself. But
when I removed the plug, water spread over the floor in a flood.
It was annoying, but not terminal – I mopped up with a towel
and we went out for a snack.

We found a decent looking bar, quieter than the others we'd
passed in which the patrons struggled to find an inch of standing
room. It even had clean linen tablecloths and a fine display of
shellfish, cheeses and hams. We ordered a small plate of
prawns, some delectable ham and two *copitas* of fino, almost
the standard order in this city of sherry and shellfish. We
enjoyed the snack and the opportunity for a relaxed rehash of
our day, but when James called for *la cuenta* his face paled
visibly.

'Look at this, we must have got the wrong bill.' He handed
it to me and I saw that it was approximately what we would
spend on the weekly shop if we had guests. I studied it: the total
was added correctly, it was just totally extortionate. We called
the waiter and questioned the prices for *tapas*.

'But, Señores, you ordered *raciones*, which cost much more
than *tapas,* and that was the finest Pata Negra ham,' he sneered,
with a 'make my day' expression. His explanation was glib and
practised – this was certainly not the first time he'd had this
dispute. We argued in vain that we'd asked for *tapas* and hadn't
specified that we wanted the most expensive ham in the world.
The bar was a tourist trap and we'd been fairly and squarely
suckered. It hurt, and not only financially.

It had been a long day, so we were in bed by midnight and
lay sweating in the fetid airlessness that sat on the chest like an
sumo wrestler after a hard bout. A gentle buzz of conversation
susurrated, not unpleasantly, somewhere close by, but I

couldn't drop off. The volume knob turned relentlessly and by three o'clock, the susurration had segued into a convivial roar, punctuated by screams of laughter and the chinking of glasses. Dragging myself out of the sopping bed, I looked down at the street to see about 100 young people doing what they do best: talking, smoking and drinking, as they put the world to rights. We hadn't really noticed the bar next door to the hotel, but clearly it was one of the most popular in the *barrio*. It continued to be popular until around four thirty, when blessed silence fell and we slid into a deep refreshing sleep... only to be awoken at 5am by the bin men arriving to empty a vitreous Niagara of bottles into their dustcart.

The next day was searingly hot, like the day before and the day after. If Madrid is the oven of Spain, Seville is the hotplate, and after a couple of hours we were done to a turn, frazzled and red-eyed, as we'd never quite achieved the Spanish knack of doing without sleep in summer. The shops had nothing but Lycra Spandex hip-hop kit, rather than the cool cotton summer dress I'd set my heart on, so after a tour of the city's architectural wonders and a good lunch we were glad to return to the homeliness and comparative cool of La Cabra.

Quickie was ready to fly, but Seville was too far to make it a realistic base, so we decided on Antequera, 90 minutes away, where there was a small flying club. The next weekend James and Brian decided to take the microlight and check it out. I had to stay at the *finca* as we had guests, which was just as well as it turned out.

The boys came back looking exhausted and distinctly guilty on Sunday evening, which made sense when they described their Saturday night out on the town. Arriving in Antequera after dark, they'd found the hotels full, but located a small busy-looking place in a back street that had a room.

'We'd like a double room with bath please,' said Brian.

'For you two *caballeros*?' enquired the man behind the desk.

'Yes, twin beds please,' affirmed Brian.

'For the whole night?' The man raised his eyebrows.

'Yes, just for one night,' Brian confirmed, thinking he had heard wrongly or misunderstood the question.

The man shrugged. 'Okay, that will be 20,000 pesetas, payable now.'

It was expensive – very expensive for a two-star hotel – but it was late and they were too tired to argue. Grumpily they paid up and were given a room key. Switching on the light revealed a chandelier-hung room tastefully furnished in pink satin, with gilt vases of florid artificial roses on every piece of furniture. Chucking the profusion of ruched cushions on the floor, they hurriedly undressed and clambered into bed.

A tapping on the door awoke them.

'*Quien*... er, whooser?' grumbled James resentfully, but the only answer was a chorus of giggles. He went to the door and peered around it, to see two dark-haired girls whispering outside. 'Sorry, wrong room,' he said, shutting the door and going back to bed.

'Whassamatta?' mumbled Brian.

'Dunno, jussa cuppla girls got the wrong room.'

Their sleep was frequently interrupted throughout the night – the hotel seemed very noisy – with slamming doors and the constant whoosh of flushing toilets.

The morning light brought a better understanding of the nature of their 'hotel'.

๛

My ma hadn't so much bitten the bullet as swallowed it and had opted to sell most of her furniture and move into a tiny cottage with her dog and cat. James agreed that he needed a holiday and he combined seeing friends with helping her move.

It seemed strange to have the house to myself, with only the cats for company, and they took full advantage of it. It was unwise to doze off in a chair with a cat on one's lap, as the other three would jump on top of the sleepers, causing a Krakatoa of raging feline jealousy and spite that left bleeding claw marks on the thighs and arms of the object of their 'affection'. It was difficult to sleep at night for the same reason. Since returning from England I'd slept on the floor, but my back was taking a long time to improve and James was also having bad back problems. Our fitful sleep was mostly thanks to Muppet – who could open the bedroom door – sneaking in to touch one's face with a paw. This made me extremely nervous and I'd leap up with a scream, which of course awoke James. Muppet would also bring in little presents: when James awoke one morning to find a tarantula nestling in his damp, musty bedclothes, we decided this camping on the floor had to stop. Ulla had left us a saggy, old iron bed with a mesh base that looked as if it was made out of discarded knight's outerwear. We threw it out and decided to make a bed. Or at least I decided and poor James had to make it.

Damp was a constant problem due to ground water flowing under the bedroom floor, causing the tiles to buckle and heave. It seemed like a good idea not to delve too deeply into the matter of renewing the floor – a huge job – so we ignored the damp. James built a splendid slatted base and the money my father had left me bought a decent mattress, which of course did the job and relieved our aching backs. It doesn't matter how often the bed manufacturers tell us to change beds, it takes most people at least six months to face up to the inevitable: you need to spend big mattress bucks to cure a bad back!

That solved the ant and tarantula problem, but we went through another snake-infested period – after which the snake killing score stood at Chica one, Houdini four and us seven. Smoo wisely didn't mess with them and Muppet was too slow. Houdini was becoming an expert snake-juggler, able to keep a serpent in the air indefinitely. For some reason known only to himself, he preferred to do his act indoors. When he became bored he would simply walk away, leaving the poor jaded thing lying around, lacking the will to live but perfectly capable of fanging an unwary bare foot.

After this marathon serpenticide, I couldn't kill them anymore. The experience of cutting off a snake's head with a machete and ten minutes later seeing the obsidian eyes still following my movements and the little tongue flickering was too upsetting even for a snake hater. I started telling them in a loud voice to go away and tried not to think about how they must be multiplying in the bank under the terrace.

∾

Smoo became ill and started looking heartbreakingly elderly, his lush fur tatty and dull. I took him to the vet, who diagnosed blocked anal glands, a dodgy lung, ulcerated gums and ear mites. Smoo screamed like a fractious child all the way home and then didn't recognise his home and got in the car again. I wondered whether cats could get Alzheimer's and was depressed and missing James, who was having a good time sorting out my mother in Dorset.

The unexpected arrival of Keef and Becky cheered me up. After a fortnight camping in Portugal in torrential rain they had headed for Spain in disgust, only to have the cart spring suspension turn upside down on the rough roads near the border. Their poor old estate managed to drag its muddy, overloaded self as far as Finca Tara before dying, and the two damp and bedraggled travellers looked forward to a bit of recuperation and refettling before continuing their journey around Europe. The Ford Escort Mk I estate had been converted into a campervan, complete with shower and cooking arrangements; quite a feat in a car of that size. In between fitting gas motorbike shocks to help with the suspension problem, they began a tree tidying and cutting marathon down on the land, so we'd be well prepared for winter fires by the time James returned.

The weather was clear and brilliantly autumnal, so we went up to Antequera. My first flight was with a Spanish instructor who didn't speak English, and I felt as nervous as an angel with no wings. The flight went well until he asked me to land

Quickie. For the first time I felt real fear and asked him to do the landing.

Rafael shook his head. *'No es posible*, Alex, you are flying well, just a little out of practice. You have control!'

'No, Rafael, I don't feel confident. I've forgotten everything. I can't do it... Look, my hands are shaking!' We were sinking fast and because *neither* of us was flying her, Quickie was all over the sky. Rafael looked bored and started examining his nails with meticulous attention, his hands ostentatiously clear of the dual-control joystick. The iron-hard ground was approaching fast, much too fast, and we needed to skew around into the wind, a touch of right rudder, throttle open just so. Rafael's horrible technique worked: instinct and training took over and, without thinking, I coaxed her onto the runway and we bumped to a halt in front of the hangar.

Keef also owned a microlight that had been languishing in a shed for years, and we had a wonderful day indulging our flying fantasies over the olive and almond-tree-studded plain, looking down on the 5,000-year-old dolmen tombs to the west of the mediaeval town and circling La Peña de los Enamorados. This strange limestone crag soars 2,500 feet into the air from the tortilla-flat plain and is shaped like an Indian face. The legend goes that a Christian man fell in love with a Moorish girl from Archidona and when their forbidden love affair was discovered, they were driven to the top of the cliff by soldiers. Rather than be parted, they embraced and leapt to their deaths together.

At the end of a perfect day I knew I wouldn't fly any more: I'm no Duchess of Bedford and it's best to go out on a high note. When the Antequera Club made me an offer for Quickie I quickly agreed – being a rare two-seater she was perfect for teaching, and it was time for other people to have the fun and deep satisfaction of soaring through the sky with 500ccs of thrashing tin and a shred of canvas strapped to their backs.

By the end of September James was home, having sorted out my mother's cottage. The lawns were covered with diaphanous spider web in the pearly early morning light, the snakes had retired to their winter quarters or been juggled to death, and the house needed its autumn clean. This isn't quite as thorough as a spring clean, more a paring back of the cobwebs that hung in wavery sheets from ceilings and light fittings, giving the place a pleasingly gothic touch. After a two-day marathon of dusting, polishing and scouring, throwing the cats into outer darkness together with their beds, our beds and any festering laundry that was beyond washing, I put on makeup and fresh clothes and limped into the hall to await the arrival of the expected guests. The scent of flowers picked from the garden trailed deliciously across the nostrils, mixed with enticing aromas from the kitchen. James arrived home with his head on one side, looking like a parrot with tendonitis after a day rewiring a basement two inches shorter than him, and we waited together... and waited. When our guests were three hours overdue, James had the good idea of checking the diary, only to discover they were due on this date... in October, a month later.

The season was definitely on the turn and midnight swims to cool down were replaced by reluctant swims in the afternoon to get fit, although visitors still found it pleasantly warm. Keef and Becky went to Morocco for a week to test the new suspension and, in the space of that week, we went from refusing to work in the afternoon due to the heat to needing the hall log-burner going all day.

The whole garden had a wonderful second flowering, which made pruning difficult – it seems downright ungrateful to hard prune something that's flowering its little heart out. The canna lilies were tall coral spears in their bronze leaves, the tree of heaven's orchid-like flowers wafted a delicate scent and even the roses were better than the spring flush as there were fewer pests.

James's basement job had turned into a whole house job, which was taking longer than it should, largely due to his being blinded by lust every time he looked out of the window and saw his employer's nubile daughter and her friends getting an all-over tan around the pool.

Traudl went to England to be with Eugene and we received a slightly worrying postcard to say her plane was late because the pilot got lost.

The autumn schedule of unannounced power cuts commenced; there could be one or several, lasting from a few seconds to a couple of hours, and they always came at the end of a long, hard bit of writing, but just before it had been saved, so everything was lost. After the third or fourth catastrophic loss, I was forced to find out how to save work automatically and how to make backups. This was more than the Minsk Medical Department was doing – it was reported that their computers and disks were stolen and the disks wiped clean before they were recovered, destroying the records of 670,000 radiation victims and 20,000 compensation payments!

We had a little more free time now that the garden didn't need constant watering and could wander the countryside. On a trip to Alora we stopped on a bridge over a wide but shallow river and watched a group of men fishing with hecks – shallow woven baskets on poles that have been used since time immemorial to flip fish out of the water. We could also see the inky stain of sprats and the shadowy shapes of cunning old fish lazily changing direction as they sensed their opponents, sliding past them just out of reach. I've heard fishermen say that smoking taints the bait or fly and the fish can smell it, in which case these particular fishermen didn't have a hope as they were all sucking on fags. A fat old laundress in a conical straw hat and cacophony of cardigans was scrubbing her washing with a bar of soap on a flat boulder by the river's edge, then rinsing it in a natural rock bowl and laying it out to dry in the sunshine. We could smell the tang of clean linen and olive soap.

Time stood still... until the 20th century arrived in the shape of a young man crunching over the stones to the river's edge to wash his new car, his soapy hands running over it in the loving caress of new ownership.

The ancient, fortified hilltop town of Alora had many gracious old buildings, but was perhaps a bit short on action. Like the locals, we sat at a pavement café and watched the lads in their pimped motors endlessly circulating the one-way system with bursts of violent acceleration, interleaved with cops in their clapped-out old bangers. James was waiting for the tax office to open, as he had received a rather worrying letter to say his tax returns weren't in order and a huge fine or a jail sentence was coming his way if the matter wasn't dealt with before a certain date. The date had already passed as the letter had been wandering around the countryside for weeks.

Normally our post went to a box in the post office – a large cardboard box that sat on the counter – and you riffled through the letters and packets and took your own plus your friends' and neighbours' mail. It could be tricky reading the addresses, which were covered with muddy paw prints in winter, as the *Correos* cat regarded the box as her bed. However, certain government letters were delivered to your residence or, more accurately, sort of delivered; the 'postman' merely handed them to the first local resident he met. This happened to be José el Vino's ancient arthritic dad, who didn't feel up to walking down our rough track until several days later.

Luckily the whole thing turned out to be a technical storm in a *copita* and the lady in the tax office merely handed James a pile of forms to complete in triplicate. She fed them through her computer and it was sorted. We went and had a celebratory drink, while watching a drunk dismount from his donkey on the downhill side of a path. Luckily for him you cannot pull a donk – the drunk spent several minutes scrabbling for purchase on the almost vertical slope, saved by the reins as the long-suffering beast stood stubbornly immobile.

Winter was almost upon us, but we were in better spirits than the previous winter. The house was fully booked over Christmas with 'returnees' and our finances were no worse than usual.

16.
Parrot Pie

By February, it wasn't only Murray who was going down the tubes. We were having another of our periodic bouts of poverty, in which you have the sort of conversation that ends in mutual recrimination over the purchase of a bottle of Pantene for dry or normal hair, rather than using up the remains of the cat's tick shampoo. We never seemed to be able to resolve the basic problem: that we were seriously under-capitalised.

Realistically, Finca Tara had been way too expensive in the first place, but by hiving off a parcel of land on the other side of the track, dropping the asking price for what remained and giving us a form of short-term mortgage, Ulla had clinched the deal, and we had committed every penny we had and more. The snag was that if we missed even one instalment she could reclaim the property, keep all the payments and leave us homeless, so finding the monthly repayment was the first call on any money; food and necessities came a poor second.

Ulla was a decent sort and I doubt if she would have made us homeless without serious provocation, but her lawyer was another *olla de grillos* (kettle of fish). Eduardo was a suavely nasty piece of work who seemed to go out of his way to complicate and obfuscate, delay or involute the most simple request. A dozen times he would tell us to be at his office at a certain hour (inevitably inconvenient to us) to sign papers, and a dozen times the papers would be 'delayed', 'incomplete' or 'awaiting a signature from Madrid'. Occasionally the office was shut and we would hang around for an hour or so drinking coffee and munching morosely on a bun before heading home with our tails between our legs. Every unnecessary trip to Torremolinos took half a day and cost money, racking up further fees for Eduardo, but Eduardo had Ulla's power of attorney because she was back in the States and we had to dance to his tune.

Amazingly, we had kept this up for three years and never missed a payment, although sometimes it was a desperate last-minute struggle to get a few hundred more pesetas into the account. The uncertainty of being able to make the payments and the inability to plan ahead or save anything was grinding us down, but the thing that grated most was not having that final signature that would make the place ours. It was like renting a property and all the work and money could ultimately be for someone else's benefit; the loving attention to detail, the twiddles and the hours spent gardening might prove to be a backbreaking waste of time.

We racked our brains for moneymaking schemes, but everything seemed to need money in the first place or a good dollop of criminal inventiveness. As other expats had discovered, the way to make a small fortune on the Costa del Sol was to start with a large one. James was working himself to the bone on building jobs, either for Joe or on his own, constantly suffering a dodgy back and carpal tunnel syndrome, which left him with aching wrists and numb fingers. I felt more and more that I wasn't pulling my weight financially, but didn't know what to do about it because the available jobs were mostly on the coast and/or unsuitable for one reason or another. Trawling through the jobs column the choice was:

1. Topless waitress/dancer
2. Barmaid
3. Secretary
4. Timeshare tout
5. Tart
6. Groom

I went through the list conscientiously, considering the pros and cons of each job and my qualifications to succeed, but the results weren't encouraging. A few minutes thought and a critical look in the mirror confirmed the worst.

1. My boobs aren't big enough and I can't dance.
2. My boobs aren't big enough and I can't count.
3. My boobs aren't big enough and I can't do shorthand.
4. My boobs aren't big enough and I can't bullshit.
5. My boobs aren't big enough and my back would kill me.
6. Okay in the boobs department but every muscle in my body would kill me.

It looked like I'd have to stick with Plan A and carry on with guests.

People who found a genuine niche in their chosen area and had selling skills could do well on the Costa, even make serious money, despite the thickets of bureaucracy seemingly designed to prevent foreigners from succeeding. A couple I knew had the idea of importing English kitchen gadgets and a limited range of 'must have' foods such as mushy peas, Branston pickle and Marmite. Pat had been a black cab driver in London and had kept on his licence, popping back to London for a cab-driving stint when cash ran low. Pat and Neva had worked the markets in their youth and the Eastender work ethic came in handy in Spain. They were the most generous people on earth and their humour and common sense helped keep us sane, as well as showing everybody that you could succeed despite advancing years and no language skills or business training.

There were always quite a number of 20 or 30-year-old villas needing rewiring. As with Finca Tara, the original wiring had been done by unqualified Spanish 'electricians', who had been picking olives for a living the previous week. To be fair, they learned quickly, but the general opinion at the time had been that a single bulb hanging from roughly the middle of the ceiling and one power point per room were quite sufficient. Putting the switch anywhere near the door was not only totally unnecessary, but probably also suspiciously limp-wristed. Behind the door was fine and had the added advantage that you could practise falling over the furniture and stepping on the cat's tail *before* your eyes failed. Modern, power-guzzling halogen stoves and electric fires were quite a problem, as foreigners couldn't understand that these appliances sometimes used more power than was coming into the house. James was constantly being called out to see to exploding fuse boxes and it frequently turned into a more lucrative total rewire when he explained the problem.

One such job was for Irish Jim in Torremolinos. He and his wife Betty lived in a comfortable old villa with their dog, cats and a gorgeous, highly loquacious green-winged macaw. The bird was an excellent mimic and kept the other pets constantly on the run by whistling, calling their names and making Betty's 'food' noises. They never seemed to learn, but at least it kept them fit. The bird could also imitate the rusty creak of the outer security steel door, cars, Jim's constant tuneless whistling, bits from radio programmes and countless other trifles. At first, James didn't find it too bad, as the parrot only spoke to people it knew, but after a few days it knew James and greeted him on arrival. He didn't care overmuch for the bird as it took an evil delight in making a raucous remark just as he was making a difficult connection, completely ruining his concentration.

Jim would usually cover the cage when they went out, but on one occasion he hadn't bothered and the bird was on top form. It copied James when he whistled through his teeth, making the setter burst into the room looking for attention. It copied him as he muttered various calculations. It copied the whine of the drill. It copied the bad language as yet another bit broke in the concrete wall. It copied the ringing of the telephone. It copied the cats meowing. It copied the scratching of blade on wood as he sharpened a pencil. It copied everything, in fact, with the perfect, pin-sharp reproduction of Bang & Olufson.

When the poor tortured red setter burst into the room for the third time to a whistled command, James snapped: advancing on the bird with an evil scowl and raised fist, he shouted: 'Why the f**k don't you shut up, you flea-ridden birdbrain?'

The parrot shuffled uncomfortably to the far end of its perch and drew a wing over its head, peeping enticingly through the feathers.

'Do you like parrot pie?' it enquired in a worried tone.

James cracked up, but wasn't going to let the parrot off that lightly. 'Yeah, I *love* parrot pie, yummy, my favourite meal!' He rubbed his hand over his stomach and stood menacingly close, pulling the cover over his tormentor after another meaningful leer at the macaw.

Jim and Betty were puzzled when they came home to find their pet unusually quiet and withdrawn, not even offering his usual query of 'Would you like some help with the shopping, love?' as Betty hauled the supermarket bags in. James didn't have the nerve to tell them about the ridiculous conversation. But he'd discovered that a leer and a rotating hand over the stomach were enough to keep it quiet.

The macaw was allowed to fly free in the house as the cats posed no danger to the big bird and, one day, the inevitable happened: a window was left open and Polly was off. Irish Jim was on crutches at the time, having fractured an ankle, and the poor man hopped for miles looking for his pet. Neighbours said they had heard it talking to itself as it creaked overhead in the awkward tail-down parrot flight, but it was nowhere to be seen. It was feared that it had been caught by someone or something, or had joined one of the flocks of escapee naturalised parrots that brighten Malaga's skies.

The old couple were bereft, although James and the setter weren't altogether unhappy about its departure. A good week later, Jim was in the garden when he heard the familiar slam of his car door, followed by the screech of the security grill and the rattle of the front door handle. Knowing Betty was indoors, he looked up, hoping against hope, and there was Polly perched in a palm tree, calmly regarding him with a bright, knowing eye, apparently none the worse for his holiday. Jim coaxed the bird down and crutched into the house with the flamboyant green and scarlet tearaway preening on his shoulder. James rather cattily remarked that he only needed an eye patch and tricorn hat and there wouldn't have been a dry eye in the house.

James was glad to finish the job as the daily 14-mile journey on Billy Goat – occasionally accompanied by a bag of cement or roll of cable – was getting him down and the parrot was sandpaper to his frayed nerves. I was nervous that one day things would get out of hand, leading to a headline in *Sur in English* along the lines of: ELECTRICIAN IN PARROT BLOODBATH HORROR.

My mother found my letters about our struggles amusing, but she was also sympathetic because she and my father had experienced much the same hand-to-mouth existence throughout their farming life. It was only when they retired to Dorset that my father suddenly found that he had a bit of a flair for playing the stock market and had gradually built up a little fund of 'rainy-day money'. Now that his estate had been settled, my mother found, for the first time in her life, that she had more than enough for her daily existence, with a few treats thrown in. We were overcome when she wrote to say that she'd like to help by buying a share in the *finca*, which would mean we could finally pay off Ulla. Of course, we'd be paying my mother a monthly income instead, but it was a lower amount and with any luck she wouldn't throw us out if we missed a payment. And if we couldn't hack it, the house would be sold and she would get her money back. This didn't solve our problems, but it did lighten them, and we tried to cheer up about our inability to become rich entrepreneurs.

It was at this dangerous moment of seeing a tiny chink of light at the end of the tunnel that Telephone Tina first appeared in our lives, in a whirl of blonde curls and six-inch killer heels, hauling a selection of radio telephones from her mud-spattered four-track.

'What a *lovely* place, Georg told me how to find you,' she trilled. 'He thought you might be interested...'

Inviting her into the kitchen for coffee, we examined some leaflets while she told us her life story – or at least the last few years of it – during which she and her husband had been building houses in the south of England.

'We just had to leave England, as John couldn't stand it a moment longer. Can you believe three lots of foundations washed away in floods in one year? He sold the business and our lovely Elizabethan house and we retired here.' Tina looked down at her immaculate red nails as the unspoken question hung in the air.

Large, hazel eyes crinkled ruefully. 'It's a bit complicated, but we lost nearly everything when the dollar crashed. My husband has been trying to sell our bananas from the *finca*, but nobody will buy them. They're the wrong shape or something, so I've been selling these phones to expats desperate to keep in touch with their families and businesses. It was lucky I had a contact who could supply them.'

'Have you sold many?' I asked. 'They aren't exactly cheap...'

'Actually, sales have been amazing,' Tina smiled. 'I mean, what choice do people have? It's human nature that if you want something, you're more likely to do business with the guy that you can speak to. It's this or nothing. Telefonica doesn't give a toss. They get their money either way. I don't make a huge profit and it's hard graft, but who knows? If it takes off I might be able to afford a horse again...'

We sighed in moist-eyed unison. Both of us missed our horses.

She was right. James had a posse of clients who'd drive over and leave a message that they needed help, but of course he couldn't advertise his skills in the local newspaper. And there was an increasing number of English craftsmen living in town who *could* get a line from Telefonica, so he was losing out twice over.

'They palm off everybody living in the *campo* with the 'Maybe next year you'll get a line' story,' Tina confirmed. 'It's one of Spain's biggest companies. They spend 60 million a year telling you to get a phone and keep in touch, and about six million putting in infrastructure. Still, silver linings and all that...I'll run through the models that might suit you.'

She brought out three radio telephones. 'Now this little beauty is a bit pricey at £3,000, but it does everything except open the door in a white lace cap. It runs an answer machine, fax, computer link and has every available bell and whistle. The middle one is more reasonable at £1,700 and has lots of features and a really good standby time...'

My heart sank; they were completely out of our reach.

'... and the junior model, which has some useful features, like rapid dialling and a running total of what a call is costing per minute, only has 12 minutes talk time, but, hey, who needs to talk for more than 12 minutes?'

I thought gloomily of Willem, who could talk about his editing needs for an hour at a stretch.

'And it comes in at a very reasonable £1,300.'

That was about £1,000 more than we could afford, but it was tempting. It was a fraction of the size and weight of Nigel's – a house brick rather than a breeze block – and the performance was surprisingly good.

'Okay, we'll have one...' I heard my tremulous voice agree to the sale. Tina put on some lipstick and zipped her bag. Suddenly we were phone owners and had joined the 20th century, and Tina was one sale closer to becoming the greatest female success story on the Costa del Sol.

The next crisis was with our Fiat 128, which had disembowelled itself for the third time, ruining yet another set of driveshafts in the process. She was just too fragile for our rutted, potholed roads and even getting it through the TVE (Spanish MOT) was a problem requiring exact timing, as there was a roving fault in the lighting system that James couldn't quite lay his screwdriver on. One or more of the lights often wouldn't work at all, which meant going out in the morning and trying them all. On the morning that they all worked, you drove gingerly into Malaga to the TVE.

This time the lights worked, but ironically it failed because the beams were pointing up in the air as they always had, the previous owner having broken off the adjustment lever. Usually we got away with it, but this time we scored a keen young mechanic looking for trouble. We drove away dejectedly, but then James smiled and swerved into a filling station. We drove out again, the 128 looking like a pimped kid's special with it's arse in the air, the front tyres almost flat and the rear ones pumped up to bursting point. This time the lights passed with flying colours, but the writing was on the wall and we started looking for something a bit more robust.

Having had a succession of Renault 4s, which are as strong as tanks and cheap to run, I fancied another one, and we went to see a suspiciously cheap one advertised at Lew Hoad's Tennis Club.

On the phone it had sounded ideal. 'I want to sell it because it isn't big enough for my dogs. It's only a couple of years old, immaculate, a real bargain,' enthused the lady owner.

One glance and we nearly walked away: the poor, sad thing was dropping to pieces at the kerb. There wasn't a single undamaged panel on the entire car. Even the roof was creased and the seats had been gnawed down to the wire underpinnings by something with large teeth. The wheel trims were crumpled foil on different sized wheels that flopped akimbo against the kerb. It didn't come as too much of a shock to discover that the owner was an astigmatic Irish lady with a poppy-red nose and two mastiffs.

'Um, how do you open the bonnet?' We'd struggled for ages to remember where the carefully concealed latch was hidden.

'Don't know me darling, can't be doing with all that mechanical nonsense! Would you like a little drinkie?'

The instruction book and papers were long gone, no doubt shredded by a terminally bored dog, but finally James prised open the bonnet to find it really was a late model with no obvious engine problems, so we bought it. Luckily the four corner panels weren't too much money and, after a session in the paint shop and the installation of Renault 5 seats from a junkyard, we had a smart and useful little car. James's big moment came when he parked in Marbella next to an immaculate new Mercedes roadster – James's radiophone started ringing and the Merc owner picked up his car phone. 'Hello, hello, who is this? Hello?...' his bronzed face creased in puzzlement at the silence on the airwaves. James waved the receiver at him and his confusion turned to a mixture of amused acknowledgement and sour lemons. Boys' toys lose their gleam when the peasants have them also!

It was just as well we hadn't used all the cats' tick shampoo, as there was a plague of them, just as two cat-loving ladies arrived for their holiday. March had come in like a lion and it was cold and wet, with wreaths of grey cloud hiding the mountains and making everything damp and sticky. We lit all the fires and our two ladies spent their days eating heartily, going on chauffeured trips with James to Ronda and Granada, reading and cat fondling. It was the cat 'lap rugs' that caused the trouble of course: they picked up ticks every time they went outside, like kids pick up head lice, by natural osmosis. Despite daily grooming and a weekly shampoo in the bidet that left me exhausted through loss of blood from multiple lacerations, the cats were a constant source of fleas and ticks, especially Smoo. It was difficult to say whether it was his lush fur, rich English blood, or the incredible savagery of his counter-attack when plonked in the bidet, but he was the main offender. Naturally, he was also the ladies' favourite lap rug, and it was a major embarrassment when Rachel felt a lump on her neck.

'Oh my dear, I *do* believe I may have acquired a parasite,' she tinkled as I got a jar of Vaseline, the tweezers and a reviving pot of Earl Grey tea. The general idea of the Vaseline was that if you smear ticks with grease they can't breathe through the spiracles on their sides, get dizzy and drop off. Pulling them off isn't recommended, as the head, which is by now anchored deep in your epidermis by steel hooks round the mouth parts, may break off and cause serious infection. Nobody had explained this to the ticks, who seemed perfectly happy to hold their breath indefinitely, or perhaps they can breathe through their bottoms if push comes to shove. After 45 minutes of Vaseline dabbing even the imperturbable Rachel – who had thoroughly enjoyed a Good War – was looking a bit fraught as the mouth parts of her own personal parasite shifted to get a better purchase. Smoo was ejected from her lap for the first time as his back legs rotated like a frenzied cyclist, sending another shower of hungry, dispossessed ticks into the air. Trowelling on another glob of Vaseline, I tweezered the swelling blob, gave a panicky tug and we both sighed with relief as the tick came away in one piece, its legs rotating wildly, just like Smoo's. For a moment I wondered whether the tick had parasites feeding on it in turn, but that way lay madness. Dropped on the fire it made a satisfactory popping noise.

Rachel was the daughter of the founder of one of our major aerospace companies and her companion ran Dick Francis seminars, so they were an amusing pair who could spin some great yarns. We invited Rick and Joan, who had a house on the outskirts of La Cabra, for supper one evening so they could share their memories. Rick was a retired airline pilot who was on the London-Cape Town route in the '30s. The evening resulted in endless reminiscences of strange and defunct aircraft in that wonderful period when the industry was reaching for the skies, cosseting air travellers with meals cooked on board, followed by a good night's sleep in a proper bed.

The ladies made a trip to Gibraltar, which they hadn't seen for 40 years, dropping me off near Marbella at David and Jill's house to finish some decorating work. The clouds had evaporated at last and it was a spring day of piercing sweetness as I walked up the mountain behind their house with my lunch. In the company of lizards, I lay warming my bones on a large, flat rock overlooking Marbella and the amethyst Mediterranean beyond. Swifts scythed like mezzaluna knives overhead as they fed on the clouds of insects. The white farmhouses tucked into the deep-folded valleys, still in their green winter pelt over ochre bones, drowsed unchanging in the sun. Many of them didn't even have a track, just the mule-paths of another century. Jays scolded and 1,000 feet below the chink and crunch of a man splitting wood rose, crisp and explicit as conversation. A raven eyed a couple of saffron butterflies and two Bulgari vulgar dung beetles fought over a particularly desirable piece of excrement. The primal scents of woody herbs and wild garlic ebbed and flowed with the breeze; medicinal, healing, excellent flavouring for a poor man's stew of rabbit, wild bird or roots. Ten miles from the heart of Marbella and I lay for a dreaming hour in the dark ages, utterly happy.

When James and I awoke the next morning, he had three blood-filled sacs like damaged thumbnails stapled to his neck, and I had one on a very personal part of my anatomy. Manfully wrenching them off himself between thumb and forefinger, he was deeply unsympathetic to my running around the room naked trying to see the bloodsucker in a hand mirror, screaming hysterically and demanding a gynaecologist...

17.
A Literary Soiree

Fat Freddie and Felicity moved from the apartment in Fuengirola – scene of the heroic rescue by the mountain rescue, police and fire departments – to their newly-built house, one of the two houses shoehorned onto a tiny plot they'd bought on the hillside above Alhaurin el Grande. It had worked out pretty well: he'd sold one house to finance the other. Their kitchen was unfinished and the water and electricity were illegally connected (they were still on the builder's licence), but Freddie didn't have time for the niceties of bureaucracy.

The doctors had treated Freddie's brain tumour as far as they could, and for two years he had enjoyed some quality of life. He and Felicity were eager to move into the house they had designed for themselves and enjoy the time Freddie had left. James and I tacked bookshelves to walls and painstakingly hung Freddie's excessively large art collection. He was a talented amateur watercolorist – particularly fond of painting local birds – and he must have had a couple of hundred bird miniatures. A batch would be chosen and hung with mathematical precision to everyone's satisfaction, but next day it was nearly always 'Um, I'm not sure about those pictures... the light's not quite right... I think the Sheppard baobab tree would look better there.'

Freddie became distressed if his increasingly microscopic view was questioned, so we'd take everything down, fill the holes, put up a different set of pictures and so on. Of course it was the tumour talking, so we all had to grin and bear it.

The house was sandwiched between the equally new mansions of two warring Welsh families locked in a permanent bad tempered Eisteddfod, in which the lads from the valleys alternately bought bigger and better sound systems to outplay the other. Their musical tastes coincided – but not with Freddie's – and sometimes it was impossible to sit on the terrace without feeling trapped in some nightmarish music festival as the heavy-duty machinery was ramped up to full capacity, accompanied by the howls from dogs for miles around.

But it wasn't so much the sound effects that worried Freddie and Felicity as the spring weather turned summery, it was the unmistakable stench of raw sewage teasing our nostrils as the adiabatic breeze blew morning and evening. Freddie squarely blamed the Welshmen for their shoddily installed waste systems and complained daily, demanding that they call in builders and dig bigger soakaways in the rocky hillside.

'These Welsh boyos are completely ignorant about building houses you know,' Freddie lectured. 'Now, when we were in Africa we learned how to design proper sewage systems – you have to have x foot of soakaway per y chamber capacity you see...' Freddie pulled down a huge book entitled *How to Design & Build Community Drainage Systems*, published in Cape Town in 1952. 'Look, here you are, this is what they should have.' He pointed at a schematic covering about five acres and featuring a settlement lagoon and reed beds.

Every time we met Freddie gave us his opinion on why the Welshmen should be denounced and forced to comply with South African regulations, and we nodded agreement, but it was worrying because the situation was becoming tense. The neighbours knew about Freddie's health and weren't unkind – and the sewage problem wasn't even theirs, as we soon discovered.

For some reason James decided to have a look into Freddie's *pozo negro*, and immediately alarm bells started ringing: the chamber was as dry and dusty as an Egyptian tomb. A bit of ferreting around the foundations of Freddie's house and the almost unbelievable truth oozed out: the builders had forgotten to connect the waste pipes to the *pozo*.

'Felicity, Felicity, psssst, come here, I've found, er, something,' James hissed. 'I don't know what we're going to tell Freddie, but the smell is nothing to do with your neighbours, it's a bit closer to home.'

Felicity was pleased that the problem was out in the open, so to speak, and the neighbours were delighted that it wasn't their fault after all. Freddie wasn't convinced.

'It's irrelevant: I'm sure my pipes have absolutely nothing to do with the smell, it's just that they don't understand how to design these things, any old rubbish will do,' he fumed. 'I may have to go down to the Town Hall and denounce them. That'll make these Welsh boyos pull their socks up and stop spreading shit all over the countryside...'

James and I slipped quietly away, wondering how Felicity was going to cope in the coming months.

At least Freddie's builders' hygienic oversights could be put down to finishing a project at excessive speed. Some American friends had been self-building with a little help for eight years and the sloth-like progress was so familiar to them they were blissfully unaware that they lived on a building site. Visiting them was an adventure that started in the roiling smoke and flames of the Tip Road, followed by a short bumpy stretch through avocado groves and someone's back yard, drawing up in front of the brutal, concrete façade of a modernistic Californian cottage. It was like stumbling over a jungle-draped, Mayan temple in the middle of Slough: slightly creepy and definitely otherworldly and more than a little dangerous, as it was full of concealed slit trenches, half-finished staircases and services hanging liana-like in the greenish gloom. Indiana Jones in mind, we kept our wits about us in order to reach the tiny, half-completed wing where they lived and worked in two rooms (plus a marble bathroom large enough to host a party). Cabot had been a hospital architect in California and Liane a teacher, but their orderly Californian lifestyle had been consumed by the quest to build their Spanish Dream House.

To begin with, Cabot had employed a building team, and they had laid foundations and created the great sweeping facades in the first three years or so. Then the Malaga College of Architects, through whom all plans must pass, had done a double take on one of their aerial mapping passes: this was no retirement *casita extranjero*, this was foreign, architectural Miguel-taking on the grand scale. The plans Cabot had submitted weren't exactly those he was working from: somewhere, flights of fancy worthy of Gaudí had crept in. They started picking apart Cabot's exquisitely detailed plans, all drawn to American standards. The flow of money slowed to a dribble, hit by the same dollar crisis that had affected Telephone Tina and her husband. If he was lucky, Cabot could afford a couple of *peones* two half-days a week. Even by his optimistic calculations, it was going to take another 14 years to finish the house. Objets trouveés of broken millstones, curiously-shaped pieces of olive wood and goat skulls lay under a unifying layer of dust, their outlines softened by sheets of spider web and the interesting, organic greeny-browns of algae.

'James and Alex, you must come to our literary tea on Sunday, it's going to be such fun!' Liane was, rightly, in no way apologetic for the way they lived, and they enjoyed a social life based on their active Christian faith. As James and I weren't into that scene, we didn't see a lot of them socially. But a literary tea sounded great and others we knew would be going, so there would be no lack of entertainment. Sunday morning dawned bright and warm, so we forsook our usual winter jeans and woollies, donned our Sunday-best summer clothes and set off for The Temple of Doom. The tea and reading was taking place on the flying deck, a huge concrete terrace with a swooping sail-shaped roof at the top of the house, enjoying a panoramic view of the surrounding countryside. It was thronged with eager literati, who, like ourselves, had taken a bit of trouble to have a wash and put on something clean and summery. After introductions to an Idaho professor of English and his wife – the stars of the afternoon's entertainment – Liane and her helpers started handing around the eats.

'Oh feck, look what I've done,' exclaimed a guest as the feather light avocado bouchée in her hand exploded down her white blouse. Soon a chorus of exclamations marred the enjoyment of the delicious avocado mouthfuls as they squirted and plopped, squished and dripped down our best clothes, followed by creamy prawn confections and a chopped tomato and olive tapenade on tiny biscuits which had unfortunately softened to the point of disintegration.

'Bloody hell, I'm freezing my b***s off,' Jack whispered at the top of his voice, 'and I can't manage these sodding little butchers. Haven't they got any decent sandwiches?'

'Shush, Jack, Liane's made some lovely food... but it is a bit chilly up here, I agree,' Maud said, pulling her skirt down over her knees. We were high above the olives and avocados, catching every flurry of the mean little breeze that was scything through a space unprotected by windows, or even walls in any meaningful sense. Still, a nice cup of hot tea would put that right.

'Who's for iced tea... or we have iced coffee or squash or cola if you prefer?' Our hostess did the rounds with the drinks and ice cubes.

'I'll settle for a nice tumbler of scotch,' Jack muttered, ignoring Maud's quelling glances while trying to squeeze into a corner between two flying buttresses.

'For goodness sake, you know they don't drink, Jack,' Maud hissed warningly.

Our friend Freddie was on sparkling form, holding court as a seasoned author on a canvas campaign chair, and we dutifully gathered around while he gave us valuable insider information on how to be published.

'Ooooh, Freddie, how many books have you written and what are they about?' asked a bubbly blonde new to the area, looking adoringly at the great man.

A collective shudder went through his friends, who knew him as a man who had always wanted to write a book, a man who definitely had a book in him, but who unaccountably hadn't yet finished his *meisterwerk*. Or even started it. We rhubarbed among ourselves while Freddie rubbed his bare forearms and put on his little white cotton sun hat.

'Drat, I *knew* we should have brought our jackets.' Felicity bit her lip. 'Freddie was so sure it was going to be stinking hot. It was 82°F on the terrace this morning you know, but it *is* only the end of May.'

'Nee'r cast a clout till May be out,' we all chorused in sibylline agreement.

Liane hugged Freddie. 'Are you cold honey? I'll go and get you a cardigan.' She looked around at her guests, most of them by now goose-pimpled and turning mauve around the edges. 'Heck, maybe I'd better fetch up some more woollies – I'd ask you to come downstairs, but there isn't anywhere we could all fit in to hear Shelton's fascinating talk...'

We all murmured that we were perfectly all right really, and Liane came back with a selection of garments. James put a red shirt over his turquoise ensemble, Freddie had an apricot angora cardigan draped over his left breast and a pink one over his right breast, and the rest of us snatched whatever we could, adding bag-lady chic to our avocado, prawn and olive-smeared garments.

'Er, Liane, sorry about this, but I've just remembered I've got an important business call to make,' Jack said as he slid towards the staircase, ignoring Maud's dagger glances.

'Someone will give you a lift home Maudie. Must go.' We looked after Jack's rapidly vanishing back, envying his presence of mind and wishing we had important business decisions to make.

Liane and Cabot stood and said a few words about their pleasure at being able to persuade their intellectual author friends to tell us about their books and we sat back to enjoy some literary stimulation.

'I am an over-achiever. My wife is an over-achiever. Three of our four children are over-achievers – I told them to bring only their successes to me, not their failures.' Shelton looked around with some satisfaction as we digested this.

Was this a good or a bad thing? It sounded rather lonely being a serial over-achiever in the Potato State. It passed through my mind that Shelton and Larraine were also over-achievers with the knife and fork, and immediately felt ashamed of my shallowness. Shelton was obviously a heavy-duty intellect, judging by his string of papers on Wordsworth and the Lake Poets.

'Our youngest daughter, Aimee, chose not to tread the path of intellectual endeavour.' Shelton paused and we pondered her strength of character. 'Aimee became involved with a young man in the employ of Satan, a drug pusher.'

We hurriedly adjusted our ideas.

'For four years I battled to win my daughter back. Although she was also in the employ of Satan, I never gave up, and finally she was persuaded to come home. This book, entitled *Aimee Come Home*, is about her.'

I was beginning to feel extremely sorry for Aimee: not only had she been branded thick and a daughter of Satan, but the whole world got to hear about her lack of moral fibre. No wonder she didn't want to come home. She couldn't exactly tell papa about her success in shifting a couple of tons of crack cocaine!

Larraine now took over and told us about the disturbed children she and her husband fostered. Larraine's problem had been that she took a dislike to one of these children, which was perfectly understandable in the light of the boy's repulsive behaviour. It wasn't explained why the child didn't simply return to the reformatory. Larraine continued to foster the teenager, but became so upset by the realisation that she could dislike another human being that she had a nervous breakdown, and her book, *The Lacunae of the Soul*, was the result of her subsequent work in therapy.

We were a bit thoughtful as we drove Maud home. Our lives seemed rather dull and boring after all the literary excitement. Jack was sitting in front of the TV with the remains of a cheese and pickle sandwich in front of him.

'Did you get your call okay?' I asked.

'My call? Er, yes, thanks Alex. Very disappointed to miss the talk of course.' He patted the sofa. 'Come and sit down, have a glass of scotch and tell me all about it.'

'Mmphhhh.' Maud made a Marge Simpson noise as she stumped off to the kitchen to make a cup of tea.

18.
The Pink Palace of Jaipur

Possibly due to a tick bite, Smoo developed a serious throat infection requiring a course of expensive antibiotic injections from the vet and devoted hand-feeding with yoghurt and tiny morsels of liver. The funny thing was the sore throat didn't stop him screeching his head off from the moment he got into the car until he got out of it again. I also went down with a painful sore throat, but noted that no one hand-fed me with paper-thin slices of raw offal. James did bring me a dead dung beetle of lapidary beauty – maybe not quite as valuable as the rocks Liz Taylor would have made up into a knuckle-duster, but just as gorgeously showy, and it's the thought that counts.

The May weather continued to be capricious. Some days hot, some with the sharply unpleasant breeze that had disrupted Cabot and Liane's party. Overall it was hot enough for Antonio to start his summer regime of pumping water up from the *río* into the tank at the top level of his land to irrigate his vegetable *huerta*, a task he liked to complete by 6am – at the latest. The petrol engine that lived halfway down his well was shatteringly noisy and the well acted as a megaphone, so the whole valley reverberated to its enhanced exhaust note, a racket guaranteed to start every dog barking within miles and drown any thoughts of sleep.

Antonio went to bed when darkness fell and rose before dawn, but of course our routine, and that of our guests, didn't quite match his. Lack of sleep began to tell, to say nothing of the embarrassment of having to explain to our guests that they would need earplugs, possibly a pillow over their heads and the windows shut tightly as well. Under these circumstances, miracle-wonder-drug soporifics begin to look good to even the most pharmaceutically conservative, so I was relieved when James had a wonderful idea: going to the car breaker's yard he picked up an exhaust system with a good silencer. Breaking it to Antonio that we wanted to modify his pump was tricky and his response predictable.

'*Hombre, porque?* The engine has run like this for years, it's perfect, so why interfere with it? Why spend unnecessary money?'

James didn't labour the point that Antonio spent at least an hour every week tinkering with the bloody-minded contraption. 'Don't worry Antonio, it won't cost you a peseta, and I promise you it will run better and will be better for us, not so noisy,' James soothed him. It was too complicated to explain that it didn't run well because it was designed to work with an exhaust system and needed to have the plugs changed at least every Leap Year. Antonio was a good-natured man, so he agreed to let James tamper with his engine, accepting that we had some fussy foreign notions about noise. James spent a happy hour wedged on a tiny ledge in the tight confines of the well, barking his knuckles on the rough cut stones as he fitted the exhaust system and new plugs. A slight modification to the well house roof and he'd finished. The next morning we awoke to sunlight streaming in the window – it was 6.30 and the smooth purring of Antonio's engine was barely louder than the birdsong.

'*Eeuh, por Dios*, I can't tell if my engine is running or not, I had to go down to check it ...' moaned Antonio as he popped out from behind his mooning tree, but the twinkle in his eye said he wasn't entirely unhappy about it either.

Salvador across the valley also had long pumping hours for his artichokes and fruit trees, but as he'd installed his engine within the last ten years, it wasn't so aggressively noisy. More as a comment than a criticism, something was said about how long his pumping took, and within the hour he came leaping across the *río* weighted down with carrier bags bulging with nutty little artichokes the size of a baby's fist and luscious coral-blushed apricots. He also changed his pumping hours a bit to suit us better. This was a huge concession – farmer's working hours are written in stone, especially when, like Salvador, they also have a day job in town.

Gradually the countryside was changing around us, as the Spanish farmers realised that the European Union could be made to work very profitably for them, although most of the older and more conservative men felt that it was solely concerned with frustrating their desire to use their land the way they always had. There had been a lot of anger about the directives that made citrus fruits and olive oil increasingly uneconomic to produce in Andalucia, and it was distressing to see the spoilt fruit lying rotting under untended trees.

In every rural bar one could hear variations of the same conversation from wrinkled, mahogany-skinned men hunched over their drinks: '*Por Dios*, how are we going to live? My lemons *por ejemplo*, last year I got good money for them, this year I'm offered a handful of almonds for a crop as good as I've ever had, not a rotten one or a fly-speck among them and the oranges the same.'

'You're right, *amigo*, my olive crop wasn't worth picking this year; I got nothing, and who is buying our good oil for *céntimos*? The Italians, that's who!'

'*D'acquerdo*, I agree, they buy our good oil and add it to their muck and then sell it for prices you wouldn't believe.'

'*Es verdad*, the Italians must give gigantic bribes to those *coños* in Brussels to take away our right to grow what we have always grown, especially when it's ten times better quality than their rubbish.'

'*Si*.'

'*Si*'

'*Claro que si!*'

Our elderly neighbour *El Rata* was made of sterner stuff, and had paid one of his *niños* to read the directives and relay the relevant information; he didn't waste time and energy moaning about the price of olives. One morning we awoke to the primeval roars and crashes of earthmovers rather than the hum of Antonio's pump, and by the end of the week hundreds of beautiful old olive trees were lying wilting in the dust. On a distant hill the framework for an *almacen* (warehouse) sprouted, to accommodate the avocados that would be produced from the thousands of new trees the Rat was planting. In the fullness of time, that is, as it would be around four years before the saplings bore fruit. Meanwhile, he installed miles of snaking polyethylene irrigation lines and built a new pump house on the riverbank – thankfully for us – to house the latest in whisper-quiet electric models.

The cunning old Rat might be an illiterate peasant, but he was well and truly *enchufe* (literally plugged in, well-connected) with the system and those who administered it locally. So much European Union money was pouring into his purse that he decided it was time that his builder son Manuel moved out of the family home on the Tip Road and built his own house. The Rat gave Manuel the plot of land at the back of our house and one day the small and inoffensive *almacen* opposite our windows – used to store olives and equipment – disappeared as earthmovers levelled the site.

We had always been worried about this development right on our boundary, as building an *almacen* (which didn't need permission on a farm), was often the first step towards building a house (which did need permission, but was easier to obtain if there was an *almacen* already on the site). Luckily, Manuel was a different kettle of fish to his dreadful parent and called on us to explain his intentions, showing us the plans for the villa of his dreams for his large family. He wouldn't agree to siting the house further away from our mutual boundary for various reasons, but he did agree to minimise the nuisance by building a high wall between the properties, and to fence our garden where it bordered his track, a big improvement on the wobbly bamboo fence we'd erected.

Manuel built the substantial house with meticulous care to detail and finish, and it featured every icon of bourgeois Spanish fashion. Swarms of admiring family and friends were taken on 'the tour' and we could hear the gasps and exclamations of wonder and delight from next door as Manuel demonstrated the sparkle of the chandeliers, the gleam of the gold bathroom fittings, the fishing-rod toting gnomes surrounding the goldfish pond and the wet bar for the swimming pool. The pool divided everyone who saw it into two camps.

'*Es fantastico*,' breathed goat-surgeon Antonia, her eyes shining through the furrows of her crow's feet. 'So romantic, it's like a film star's house with that pink heart-shaped pool.'

'*Que culo*,' muttered Antonio disgustedly, 'what an asshole the man must be, wasting money like that, when a *depósito* would have done just as well.'

We were just glad that Manuel had put up a decent fence to divide his driveway from our garden, and our only regret was that he's chosen to build his house within ten feet of our back wall, despite having acres of land to play with. It did seem a bit perverse, but had more to do with the Spanish relish for living cheek by jowl with their neighbours than anything else. We nicknamed the strawberry pink edifice The Pink Palace of Jaipur; it could be seen from miles away and made a useful landmark for strangers.

෨

I thought about Robert Browning's poem, Home Thoughts from Abroad, and the homesick longing of the line:

> '*Oh to be in England, Now that April's there.*'

It was now May, but perhaps I'd been thinking about it for a couple of weeks. The thing was, he never did go back to England in April, but stayed firmly in Fiesole, sitting in the garden drinking wine and enjoying the good weather, like most expats.

The English people we met who had moved to Spain with the idea of settling seemed to fall into three main groups: those who quickly found out that they couldn't hack life away from the delights of warm beer, fast food and their mates; those who felt like Browning and occasionally visited England; and those who would mutter darkly, 'Delights? What delights? Never want to see the bloody place again.'

That said, a certain nostalgia seemed to creep in at roughly seven-year intervals, or when ill health caused problems, despite the fact that medical care is, in general, better in Spain than in England. More accurately, medical care is usually excellent, but nursing care is largely non-existent, as are care homes, because the family look after the sick and elderly. If someone has to be hospitalised, the family shock troops surge in, complete with bawling babies, friends and dogs. They feed and wash the patient, change the bed linen and dressings, collect prescriptions and stay all day and most of the night, chatting in case the afflicted one might fall asleep and get some rest.

For American expats, returning home for medical care wasn't an easy option, so when Cabot felt decidedly unwell one sweltering morning as he was planting a bed of lilies, he was taken into a Malaga private hospital and operated on within hours for a cardiac blockage. Liane managed to get the word out from Cabot's bedside and everyone rallied around, looking after their dogs, cooking tempting little dishes and offering whatever services they could. As Liane was exhausted after 24 hours without sleep, I volunteered to do night duty. The small hospital was in a quiet street bordering a leafy square in the centre of Malaga, not far from the cathedral. The imposing marble-pillared portico led into a much more domestic, even cosy atmosphere, and a nurse directed me to Cabot's pleasant room overlooking the square. Liane was so tired and worried she could barely speak as she showed me the sluice room and bedpans, kitchenette and refrigerator, and everything else needed to get through the night, before buzzing off to La Cabra in her beat-up old VW Beetle for a good night's sleep.

Cabot was conscious and smiling, but still in a lot of post-operative pain and draped with IV lines. The dressings on the huge wound on his chest looked as though they would shortly need changing, so I rang the bell. The nurse had a quick peek; nodding in agreement, she came back with some sterile dressing packs which she put on a table. Beckoning me over to the IV stand she indicated what speed the drips should be going through and wished me a cheery good night. It was only some time later, when the blood-soaked dressings couldn't cope with any more seepage, that I realised that nurse Alex was on her own. Towards morning as a drip ran low, I rang the bell and waited anxiously. Surely getting air in the line was a bit of a no-no? A yawning nurse in scrubs came in and changed it, much to my relief, as it would have been a shame to undo all that good work by pumping poor Cabot full of embolisms instead of antibiotics. Apart from getting his sheets a bit damp with the bed-bath, my shift ended uneventfully and Cabot improved rapidly. But then I knew if he survived my cups of tea – notorious worldwide for their undrinkability – he would survive anything.

In a strange way the night had been quite enjoyable and it even crossed my mind that nursing would be good career. But I didn't see how I could afford to take enough time off to train, so that was a bit of a non-starter. A job was top of the list right now. I had to find something to bring in regular money because a disaster – for once not of our own making – had struck and many of James's clients were involved.

The Bank of Commerce and Credit International (BCCI) had been offering enticingly good returns on its deposit accounts for around two years. So good, in fact, that thousands of people had invested large sums, some of them every penny that they could scrape together, even mortgaging their houses to raise extra money. The old saying, 'If it seems too good to be true, it probably is…' was conveniently forgotten by people who should have known better, as well as by the financially naïve who'd never been scammed before.

For once in our lives, James and I were glad we hadn't any spare cash to invest when the news that BCCI was in trouble hit the media and our worried friends tried to find out what was happening. Within the week it was obvious that the news was as bad as it could be, the bank was going to default and there was no safety net. Everywhere you looked there were frantic investors phoning friends and advisers, trying to find out if they would get anything back, sifting through the ruins of their finances. Two people we knew were made totally destitute and only survived on small handouts from those less badly affected. There were marriage bust-ups, suicides and businesses going under. The whole Costa del Sol was hurting and inevitably people started cancelling any job that wasn't immediately necessary, including a lot of work that James had lined up.

BCCI wasn't the only scam that came to light in those days of unregulated banking. Another fraudster offering an investment scheme with salivatingly-good returns was arrested and bail was set at the equivalent of £10,000. Nobody, bar the judge and the English press, was surprised when he skipped bail and vanished with the £2 million he'd liberated from his client's accounts.

Despite a brainstorming session over the kitchen table, we couldn't come up with a scam to part people from their money on a similar scale, so it looked like it was going to have to be a regular, cash-earning job for me.

19.
The Augean Stables

Combing through *Sur in English* for a job, I found that the selection was much the same as previously. It didn't look any more hopeful the second time around, although there was a casino advertising for croupiers. Unfortunately that also came under the 'I can't count' heading. Nothing had changed in the cleavage department, therefore there was only one possibility and I phoned the riding school.

'Er, the job advertised, for a groom, is it still available?' I asked.

'Hold on, I'll get Rose, she owns the place...' said a weary male voice, followed by retreating footsteps.

'Rose here,' said a warm friendly voice. 'So you're interested in this job working with horses. Are you experienced?'

'Yes, I'm experienced in all aspects of horse care. Can you tell me what the job involves?'

'We have 18 horses here at La Herradura, mostly our own, but a few on livery. I'm looking for someone who can do two full nine-hour days and four afternoon shifts of four to eight, mucking out, feeding, exercising and cleaning tack. Do you think you could cope with that?'

I gulped, knowing what sort of workload 18 horses meant. 'What other help do you have Rose?' I asked, expecting the worst.

'We have one other full-time groom, Phillip, and two part-timers who do a couple of hours a day and come in when we're busy or when we have a show,' Rose replied. It was, as I'd expected, the absolute minimum possible with that number of horses. 'Would you like to come and see La Herradura before you make your mind up?'

'Yes, Rose,' I replied firmly, thinking of the dreadfully uncomfortable corset and bunny ears alternative. 'I'd like to come and see you.'

A pack of dogs swirled around the car as it stopped in the yard, the mastiff-sized canines peeing on the wheels, while the terrier-sized varieties yapped and sniffed my ankles as I waded through them towards the clubhouse. The view from the terrace in front of the old whitewashed Spanish house was stunning, the ground dropping away from the far side of the big, rectangular sand manège to give a panoramic view of Malaga Bay, the city and the jagged backdrop of mountains that faded into the distance of snow-peaked Granada. Going through the door into the trophy-studded bar, there was a seating area in front of a massive fireplace, the tables covered in old copies of *Horse & Hound* and newspapers, while the TV was tuned to the BBC news. The casual homely atmosphere was underlined by a fat marmalade cat asleep on the bar counter.

'Hello, I'm Rose, you must be Alex. Come and sit down and have a drink while we talk.' I turned from tickling the cat's chin to see a beautiful, silver-haired English rose hobbling into the bar using a stick, cornflower blue eyes creased into a welcoming smile. She rummaged under the cat, who yawned luxuriously but declined to move, and produced a sheet of paper. 'This has details of the shifts. You can swap with Phillip if either of you need a particular day off, just as long as the work is done.'

The door opened and a mahogany-tanned blonde in her forties dressed in a skimpy beaded chiffon cocktail top and skin-tight jeans drifted in and plopped down in a chair. 'Hello Lois, did you have a good evening, or shouldn't I ask?' wondered Rose.

Lois rubbed smudged panda eyes and rummaged for a cigarette. 'Yeah, party was still going strong when we left. Any chance of a cuppa Rose?'

Rose waved a hand in my direction. 'This is Alex, she's here about the job. Lois is my partner in La Herradura, Alex.'

Lois yawned in unison with the ginger cat. 'Suppose I should give you a tour of the yard, Alex, but I'm sure Phillip will do it better. He knows all the details about the feeding and that...maybe I'll see you later?' She drank the last of her tea and got up. 'I'm off for a kip Rose. Oh, here's Phillip now.'

'Oy oy Lois, you lazy cow, you spend more time on the bloody tiles than these friggin cats,' he remarked with a grin. He turned to Rose, who was checking the day's lesson schedule. 'Rose, we'll need the vet to Baron, he's got an infected willy. Peque is coughing, and Illusion has a fetlock like a football.'

He turned to me, giving my physique a quick professional once-over. 'You the one I spoke to on the phone? Hope you're stopping, I could do with some help before I drop dead of friggin overwork, and these women are useless except as slave drivers.'

I laughed. 'Well, looks like you *could* be in luck Phillip... you'd better show me the horses.'

As we walked through the yard he showed me well fed and cared-for horses standing in deep clean bedding, and I knew it was going to be okay. This would be hard work, but without the added misery of working with undernourished and badly-treated animals. When we got back to the bar, John, Rose's husband, was in the kitchen.

'Hi Alex,' he grinned. 'Sit down with Phillip, breakfast is coming up.' As I sat down the marmalade cat clambered onto my lap and a lurcher stood on my foot and gazed soulfully into my eyes.

'That's TC on your lap, and Bangle living in hope that you'll have something left over,' John remarked. 'They keep turning up and adopting us,' he said, as my gaze swept over the eight dogs and three cats milling around the bar waiting for their breakfast. 'The locals know we're a soft touch and just dump animals at the gate... Come to that, I think even the strays know we're soft. Airport there just sat around looking mournful until we let him stay. They're an absolute curse,' he added, looking around fondly at the jostling mob. 'Are you going to join us here?'

'Er, yes, I think so John,' I said. There wasn't much choice really. It seemed I was already part of the family.

'Never mind Alex, if you get through the first day you'll probably live,' he grinned. 'Have another cup of tea.'

The first week was tough. Even my garden-calloused hands developed blisters carrying heavy water buckets and wheeling big manure barrows up the steep ramps from the lower level stables. Phillip was helpful and did more than his share of the heavy work, but his day off was a killer as it meant mucking out and watering all 18 horses on my own. Lois did the feeding when we were single handed, but the first day on my own I got home at dusk in a state of smelly exhaustion. James whipped up a curious meal of fried spaghetti and boiled mince, a combination which normally wouldn't have got a very good reception. But after an exhausting day it tasted like manna from heaven, and I went straight to bed with an aching back and almost frozen shoulder. But in that brief moment between the head hitting the pillow and sleep, there was a light bulb moment.

'Please Rose, John, can we have some hoses?' I asked piteously the next morning. 'James worked out we lift over two tons of water each in a week and I'm wrecked.' John went out with his tape measure and next day there were hoses, wonderful, blessed hoses long enough to reach into most of the boxes. We could now fill the buckets in situ, rather than taking the buckets to the tap. It was a triumph of brains over brawn that all the grooms appreciated. I thought for a long time about how to automate the manure run, but building a conveyer belt around the yard seemed a bit beyond us, so we had to go on doing it the conventional way, with hard labour.

In any riding school, there are popular ponies, which everyone loves and clamours to ride, and a few unpopular ones. There's usually a good reason for this. As the new girl on the block, I got to exercise the unpopular ones. I also had my first ride on Indio, a pretty but bad-tempered coloured pony who kicked and bit while being saddled and ignored his rider's commands. Riding school horses can be pretty smart at getting their own way and will try it on if you let them, so I gave him a couple of sharp taps on the shoulder with the whip. I cantered around the arena, wondering why his action felt so odd and awkward, but my attention was on Phillip, who was standing beside the railings doubled up with laughter.

'Ride 'im cowgirl!' he bawled. 'Roll-up ladies and gents, see the amazing bucking bronco!'

Now that he mentioned it, I realised that Indio's bottom was somewhere up behind my head. 'Thanks very much Phillip, what didn't you tell me?' I grumbled as we corkscrewed past.

'Only that he bucks like a rodeo pro if you use the whip!' Phillip guffawed.

Indio quickly became my favourite because he was a sweet, affectionate pony once you got to know him and a good jumper, but some people brought out the devil in him. As he was being saddled one day he kicked out and caught Phillip on the ankle, rupturing his Achilles tendon and putting him out of action for weeks. As a result, Rose sold him as the work was hard enough without the staff being crippled. I heard that he had sadly died of colic after only a short time with his new owner, a teenage boy who wanted a show jumper.

With Phillip off work I was the reluctant head groom and Rose took on a two more girls. There was a constant programme of shows and *doma*, the Spanish form of dressage, as well as the daily classes and one-on-one tuition, so we were always busy. I was looking for more income, so when Rose suggested doing some tuition in my 'spare' time, I jumped at the chance. The job of teaching very young children and first timers isn't everybody's idea of fun, but it's satisfying to see a nervous child become a confident rider. This was close to my heart as I was the frequently-terrified child of an exceptionally talented mother who could have ridden the devil himself. She never showed the slightest sympathy when I fell off or was run away with by some excitable animal that was far too strong for me. All I got was: 'Get back on at once, shorten your reins and try again.' I understood all too well the terrors of being out of control and at the mercy of a Thelwell cartoon pony a great deal bigger and meaner than myself.

My first lesson one Tuesday morning was with some young Spanish children who wanted to be able to ride in the local *feria*; it didn't start well. The ponies were at their freshest and naughtiest after their Monday day off and the kids were no better: they chattered and giggled and it took a good ten minutes to get the two little girls on the ponies – facing the ears rather than the tail – and holding the reins correctly. Their proud but anxious parents watched closely. Like all non-riders they were worried that their offspring would fall off and break their bones. The sisters needed to be on a leading rein, but the boy had been riding for several weeks and was happy to practise on his own.

To start with, everything went well and we were relaxed and having a good time. Suddenly a breeze started to blow and within minutes the gusts were swirling sand into the air, gritting eyes and making the ponies jumpy. Daisy stopped dead abruptly and, digging in her hooves, refused to budge, while Pajaro pulled away. His little rider abruptly hauled on the reins like a cowboy doing an emergency stop on the edge of a cliff. Maddened by the pain in its sensitive mouth, the pony threw up its head and lunged backwards, dragging the leading rein across the stalled Daisy's bottom. Daisy took violent exception to her anal region being violated and clamped her tail tightly over the rein, laying back her ears in warning. The two little girls bounced around and jabbered in Spanish, drumming their heels and flapping the reins, further infuriating the unhappily joined ponies, as I lifted Daisy's tail and tugged at the trapped leading rein.

Things began to go really pear-shaped as the anally retentive Daisy trod heavily on my foot, then barged into Pajaro, starting a squealing open-mouthed fight between the ponies, while the girls screeched in terror. Doubled over in pain, I had an upside-down view of Julian – who had been quietly trotting in circles at the other end of the arena – as a large piece of plastic swooped through the air and wrapped itself around Dorada's head. Dorada, usually calm and well behaved, completely lost it: she stumbled, put her head down and bucked. As Julian lost his reins and pitched screaming onto her neck, she broke into a gallop across the arena and through the gate – which should have been closed – towards the stables. Julian's mother joined in the screaming and the chorus swelled as my imagination embroidered what would happen to Julian's head and legs if Dorada carted her rider into the stable without slowing. Luck was with us; fortunately Lois had been alerted and grabbed the frightened pony as she clattered through the yard, and lifted down the wailing but unhurt Julian.

The children's mother broke her rosary and relapsed into hysterics in the excitement of nearly losing three children in one go. The father searched for his lawyer's number as he lit up his tenth cigarette, but we managed to sort things out, helped by the fact that it was father who'd left the gate open.

This experience was nearly the first and last lesson of my teaching career, but Marie and Elaine, two of the other instructors, just laughed and said worse things had happened to them. After a while, teaching became easier and one could usually guess which disaster was next on the cards.

The most difficult pupil to teach was a Finnish boy who couldn't speak English or Spanish. His father could speak English, so we would discuss what I wanted his son to do, and he would tell me the phrase in Finnish. After half an hour, my short-term memory was overloaded and the poor, confused child was ordered to tie his reins around the horse's left ear rather than to turn left. The only phrase that came to mind sounded like '*Laûken met verst!*' which I thought meant 'Trot on slowly,' but probably means 'Gallop in reverse.'

James occasionally found time to come to the stables to help me with the exercising. We would hack out into the countryside, which wasn't very exciting as it was quite built up, but it gave the horses a change of scenery which they seemed to enjoy. Often we'd pass our *abogado* Eduardo's house, a monstrous confection perched on the hillside like a discarded wedding cake, and a monument to lawyers' ability to part their suffering clients from their hard-earned cash.

Working at La Herradura was like being an extra in a long-running soap opera with a cast of characters who only needed a malicious tweak in order to spring into Technicolor immortality. The synopsis for a series was practically on its way to the BBC:

Loveable, sweet-natured Rose, 59, owns and runs La Herradura, despite being crippled with arthritis. Her partner is her model-thin, fun-loving sister Lois, 40ish, who is addicted to diaphanous garments, gin and Dale, who is Rough Trade when he isn't being a Rough Builder.

John, Rose's toy boy ex-surgeon husband, 48, loathes horses and is usually to be found on his sailboat, enjoying the company of a crew of nubile, tight-jodhpured nymphets.

T*he two riding instructors, Elaine, 24, and Marie, 34, are on bad terms with John because they are no longer invited on his boat, having passed their sell-by-date of 19.*

Marie – a feisty, curvaceous strawberry blond – has a daughter Stacey, 16, who is unsure whether to accept John's nautical invitations – despite her mother's warnings – or lavish her pubescent charms on Francisco, 19, a pustuled but well-hung Spanish boy who keeps a horse at the stables. Francisco's father Javier, 60, is Rose and Lois's accountant and has a hold over them because he knows the secret that lies behind their acquisition of the riding school.

Tiffany Taylor Hill, 28 – a beautiful American heiress who keeps her two saddle horses at La Herradura – is in New York to see her obstetrician when her husband Larry phones to ask for a divorce so he can marry his mistress Charlene, who is expecting his child. Tiffany – a recovering alcoholic who has only just returned from drying out at the Sierra Tucson – rings Elaine in floods of tears: she had just discovered that after years of trying for a baby she also is pregnant by Larry. Elaine, who is close to Tiff, jets to New York to find her friend holed up in a hotel room, sodden with tears and drink, threatening suicide.

Meanwhile, Marie's husband Terry has vanished, leaving a note saying they have lost everything in the BCCI crash and he needs a few days to think things over. Marie's hands trembles as she drops the letter. Long after midnight, Stacey's bed is still empty. Next day Marie helps Balthazar, the darkly handsome vet, as he treats Muffin, one of Tiff's horses, for bot fly. His hand touches hers and Marie's heart leaps as Balthazar mutters 'Ze loffly blond, I loff ze loffly blond.' But Lois tells Marie of her suspicions that Balthazar is gay because he hasn't taken advantage of her invitations to visit the hay store ... and Marie remembers that Muffin is a palomino – so which of them was he talking to, her or the horse?

My mother was constantly asking for updates on the developing story. 'Has Lazy Lois made it up with Dale yet after he called her a slag and pushed her into the back of his van on top of the plumbing bits when her bikini fell off at the beach party?'

'Did Marie work out whether Balthazar was gay after going to the transvestite night club in Torremolinos with him and his mates, and does the disappearance of the letter from the accountant (about BCCI) mean Terry has been home, or has the dog eaten it?

The saga had great possibilities, certainly more than *El Dorado*, the ill-fated BBC soap that had been filmed on the Costa del Sol. It folded after a year, much to the disgust of many in La Cabra who had been making a crust from it as extras and technicians.

20.
The End of the
Beginning

The weather was on the turn: inky clouds of squeaking swifts darkened the skies on their way south, while intermittent bangs and the baying of dogs heralded another hunting season. The giant hare that lived a bachelor life in the shadow of the abandoned farmhouse on the other side of the valley was an early victim. This was the hare that I'd watched all summer as it sat on its haunches contemplating its kingdom. We felt a helpless rage as the hunters moved off, its carcass hanging down the shooter's back almost to his knees. Its death, although natural enough in the rural scheme of things, affected us: it was *our* hare, part of the landscape.

The garden was blazing with the last flowering of the patriotic red and yellow bandera. Flame canna lilies nestled in their spears of bronze foliage, sky blue plumbago sang against the intensely pink and purple bougainvillea, and the scent of roses and *dama de noche* was dizzying. The grapefruit tree was loaded with pale lemon cannonballs that wouldn't ripen any further; it seemed a shame to throw them away but I couldn't think of anything to do with the pale, acidic flesh, although we made the shells into slug traps.

In the space of a week, the breathless heat of summer had crisped into autumn and we morphed from living in the garden and searching for the smallest breeze to lighting the wood burner in the hall as soon as darkness fell. The local wildlife didn't wish to contemplate death or hibernation quite yet, so every buzzing, crawling thing for miles around was trying to get indoors: the house swarmed with greenbottles and bluebottles, millipedes, centipedes, scorpions, voles and monstrous spiders which constructed hugely-ambitious webs that failed to catch any flies. Snow was falling in England, which temporarily made us feel smug, until a nip in the air and a blue cast to the sunlight highlighted the albescent peaks of the sierras above Granada.

The phone call came out of the blue.

'Hi Alex, how are you? Haven't seen you for ages. Look, we're having a little Christmas celebration and we'd like you and James to come down to Marbella. Actually we'd like to have a talk with you both.'

'Sounds great Dolores, we'll look forward to seeing you and Rodrigo. What do you want to talk to us about?'

'We'll save that for when we see you on the 27th, 'til then...'

I'd known them for many years and we occasionally met for a meal. James and I briefly wondered what they wanted to talk about. We couldn't imagine what a busy GP like Rodrigo would want from us. Maybe he wanted James to rewire the surgery, or me to paint it?

After the party, Rodrigo sat us down in a pretty sitting room filled with flowers and silver-framed photos of the family. What he had to say came as a total surprise.

'We get a lot of patients with drug and alcohol problems, and we've been thinking about opening a rehab clinic for a long time. One of the doctors in the practice has specialised in addiction. A suitable building has come up and we'll be opening in January. Dolores and I were wondering if you two would like to run the clinic?'

James and I mirrored dropped jaws and Rodrigo continued:

'We were thinking James could run the office, look after admissions and generally keep the place shipshape. Alex, you would oversee the housekeeping and the kitchen – you'd have staff of course – look to the general welfare of the patients when the nurses and counsellors left in the evening, drive them to AA meetings and the like.'

'You would have to live in – there's a separate flat,' said Dolores. 'And a vehicle, something like a Renault Espace, would be provided. Although we can't afford big salaries, we might be able to do a profit-sharing scheme later on.'

'But we don't know anything about addicts or alcoholics,' I mumbled, thinking there were advantages to a menial job that you could cope with in your sleep, rather than one where you might not be able to sleep at all!

Rodrigo laughed. 'You don't have to. Doctors, qualified nurses and counsellors will be looking after the patients and working with them during the day. When they knock off in the evening, you'll take over. But if a patient is having a problem, a doctor or nurse will be there within minutes, and a night nurse will be provided for any patient who needs specialised care. You will take them to meetings and events, make sure they have a good diet and exercise, and that the clinic runs smoothly. The counsellors will train you in every aspect of how to interact with patients, so don't worry too much about that.'

'Er, what sort of salary were you thinking of?' James asked. Rodrigo mentioned a sum that seemed like instant wealth to us. James and I glanced at each other, bewildered at the sudden change in our fortunes.

'Yes, well, thank you,' said James. 'I think we'd like to run your Clinic. We'd like that very much.'

A wave of sadness engulfed us at the thought of leaving our beloved Finca Tara, and I knew Rose and John would be upset when they heard our news. They had taken James and I under their wing and become a much-loved part of our lives. But fate sometimes lays down her cards unexpectedly. It was time to move on again, to take a different road. Had we known the nature of the road and where it was leading us, we might have paused much longer. But that's another story...

BUYING A HOME SERIES

Buying a Home books, including **Buying, Selling & Letting Property**, are essential reading for anyone planning to purchase property abroad. They're packed with vital information to guide you through the property purchase jungle and help you **avoid the sort of disasters that can turn your dream home into a nightmare!** Topics covered include:

- Avoiding problems
- Choosing the region
- Finding the right home and location
- Estate agents
- Finance, mortgages and taxes
- Home security
- Utilities, heating and air-conditioning
- Moving house and settling in
- Renting and letting
- Permits and visas
- Travelling and communications
- Health and insurance
- Renting a car and driving
- Retirement and starting a business
- And much, much more!

Buying a Home books are the most comprehensive and up-to-date source of information available about buying property abroad. Whether you want a detached house, townhouse or apartment, a holiday or a permanent home, these books will help make your dreams come true.

Save yourself time, trouble and money!

Order your copies today by phone, fax, post or email from: Survival Books, PO Box 3780, YEOVIL, BA21 5WX, United Kingdom (☎/▤ +44 (0)1935-700060, ✉ sales@survivalbooks.net, 🖥 www.survivalbooks.net).

LIVING AND WORKING SERIES

Living and Working books are essential reading for anyone planning to spend time abroad, including holiday-home owners, retirees, visitors, business people, migrants, students and even extra-terrestrials! They're packed with important and useful information designed to help you **avoid costly mistakes and save both time and money.** Topics covered include how to:

- Find a job with a good salary & conditions
- Obtain a residence permit
- Avoid and overcome problems
- Find your dream home
- Get the best education for your family
- Make the best use of public transport
- Endure local motoring habits
- Obtain the best health treatment
- Stretch your money further
- Make the most of your leisure time
- Enjoy the local sporting life
- Find the best shopping bargains
- Insure yourself against most eventualities
- Use post office and telephone services
- Do numerous other things not listed above

Living and Working books are the most comprehensive and up-to-date source of practical information available about everyday life abroad. They aren't, however, boring text books, but interesting and entertaining guides written in a highly readable style.

Discover what it's really like to live and work abroad!

Order your copies today by phone, fax, post or email from: Survival Books, PO Box 3780, YEOVIL, BA21 5WX, United Kingdom (☎/📠 +44 (0)1935-700060, ✉ sales@survivalbooks.net, 🖥 www.survivalbooks.net).

OTHER SURVIVAL BOOKS

The Alien's Guides: *The Alien's Guides to Britain and France* will help you to appreciate the peculiarities (in both senses) of the British and French.

The Best Places to Buy a Home in France/Spain: The most comprehensive homebuying guides to France and Spain, containing detailed profiles of the most popular regions for home-buying.

Buying, Selling and Letting Property: The most comprehensive and up-to-date source of information on buying, selling and letting property in the UK.

Earning Money From Your Home: Essential guides to earning income from property in France and Spain, including short- and long-term letting.

Foreigners in France/Spain: Triumphs & Disasters: Real-life experiences of people who have emigrated to France and Spain, recounted in their own words.

Lifelines: Essential guides to life in specific regions of France and Spain. See order form for a list of current titles in the series.

Making a Living: Essential guides to self-employment and starting a business in France and Spain.

Renovating & Maintaining Your French Home: The ultimate guide to renovating and maintaining your dream home in France.

Retiring Abroad: The most comprehensive and up-to-date source of practical information available about retiring to a foreign country.

Shooting Caterpillars in Spain: The hilarious experiences of an expatriate who sent to Spain in search of . . . she wasn't quite sure what.

Surprised by France: Even after living there for ten years, Donald Carroll finds plenty of surprises in the Hexagon.

Broaden your horizons with Survival Books!

Order your copies today by phone, fax, post or email from: Survival Books, PO Box 3780, YEOVIL, BA21 5WX, United Kingdom (☎/🖷 +44 (0)1935-700060, ✉ sales@survivalbooks.net, 🖳 www.survivalbooks.net).

		Price (incl. p&p)			Total
Qty.	Title	UK	Europe	World	
	The Alien's Guide to Britain	£6.95	£8.95	£12.45	
	The Alien's Guide to France	£6.95	£8.95	£12.45	
	The Best Places to Buy a Home in France	£13.95	£15.95	£19.45	
	The Best Places to Buy a Home in Spain	£13.95	£15.95	£19.45	
	Buying a Home Abroad	£13.95	£15.95	£19.45	
	Buying a Home in Australia & NZ	£13.95	£15.95	£19.45	
	Buying a Home in Cyprus	£13.95	£15.95	£19.45	
	Buying a Home in Florida	£13.95	£15.95	£19.45	
	Buying a Home in France	£13.95	£15.95	£19.45	
	Buying a Home in Greece	£13.95	£15.95	£19.45	
	Buying a Home in Ireland	£11.95	£13.95	£17.45	
	Buying a Home in Italy	£13.95	£15.95	£19.45	
	Buying a Home in Portugal	£13.95	£15.95	£19.45	
	Buying a Home in South Africa	£13.95	£15.95	£19.45	
	Buying a Home in Spain	£13.95	£15.95	£19.45	
	Buying, Letting & Selling Property	£11.95	£13.95	£17.45	
	Earning Money From Your French Home	£11.95	£13.95	£17.45	
	Earning Money From Your Spanish Home	£11.95	£13.95	£17.45	
	Foreigners in France: Triumphs & Disasters	£11.95	£13.95	£17.45	
	Foreigners in Spain: Triumphs & Disasters	£11.95	£13.95	£17.45	
	Costa Blanca Lifeline	£11.95	£13.95	£17.45	
	Costa del Sol Lifeline	£11.95	£13.95	£17.45	
	Dordogne/Lot Lifeline	£11.95	£13.95	£17.45	
	Normandy Lifeline	£11.95	£13.95	£17.45	
	Poitou-Charentes Lifeline	£11.95	£13.95	£17.45	
	Provence-Côte d'Azur Lifeline	£11.95	£13.95	£17.45	
	Living & Working Abroad	£14.95	£16.95	£20.45	
	Living & Working in America	£14.95	£16.95	£20.45	
	Living & Working in Australia	£16.95	£18.95	£22.45	
	Living & Working in Britain	£14.95	£16.95	£20.45	
	Living & Working in Canada	£16.95	£18.95	£22.45	
	Living & Working in the European Union	£16.95	£18.95	£22.45	
	Living & Working in the Far East	£16.95	£18.95	£22.45	
Total carried forward (see over)					

ORDER FORM

Qty.	Title	Price (incl. p&p) UK	Europe	World	Total
		Total brought forward			
	Living & Working in France	£14.95	£16.95	£20.45	
	Living & Working in Germany	£16.95	£18.95	£22.45	
	L&W in the Gulf States & Saudi Arabia	£16.95	£18.95	£22.45	
	L&W in Holland, Belgium & Luxembourg	£14.95	£16.95	£20.45	
	Living & Working in Ireland	£14.95	£16.95	£20.45	
	Living & Working in Italy	£16.95	£18.95	£22.45	
	Living & Working in London	£13.95	£15.95	£19.45	
	Living & Working in New Zealand	£16.95	£18.95	£22.45	
	Living & Working in Spain	£14.95	£16.95	£20.45	
	Living & Working in Switzerland	£16.95	£18.95	£22.45	
	Making a Living in France	£13.95	£15.95	£19.45	
	Making a Living in Spain	£13.95	£15.95	£19.45	
	Renovating & Maintaining Your French Home	£16.95	£18.95	£22.45	
	Retiring Abroad	£14.95	£16.95	£20.45	
	Shooting Caterpillars in Spain	£9.95	£11.95	£15.45	
	Surprised by France	£11.95	£13.95	£17.45	
				Grand Total	

Order your copies today by phone, fax, post or email from: Survival Books, PO Box 3780, YEOVIL, BA21 5WX, United Kingdom (☎/▤ +44 (0)1935-700060, ✉ sales@ survivalbooks.net, 💻 www.survivalbooks.net). If you aren't entirely satisfied, simply return them to us within 14 days for a full and unconditional refund.

I enclose a cheque for the grand total/Please charge my Amex/Delta/Maestro (Switch)/MasterCard/Visa card as follows. (delete as applicable)

Card No. _ _ _ _ _ _ _ _ _ _ _ _ _ _ _ _   Security Code* _ _ _

Expiry date _____ Issue number (Maestro/Switch only) _____

Signature _____ Tel. No. _____

NAME _____

ADDRESS _____

_____

* The security code is the last three digits on the signature strip.